Lorraine V. Murray tells ᵃ
could face the cross of ca
learned from her suffering ..... others once she put
Christ "in the driver's seat." This is a moving, practical,
very spiritual encounter between the writer and the
reader.

ANTOINETTE BOSCO
author *of Shaken Faith: Hanging in There
When God Seems Far Away*

In her wonderfully practical and profoundly spiritual
book, Lorraine Murray often refers to the light of Christ
piercing the darkness of cancer. Her book itself
exemplifies that light. *Why Me? Why Now?* is a must for
all who feel overwhelmed by darkness.

MARCI ALBORGHETTI
author of *A Season in the South* and *Freedom
from Fear: Overcoming Anxiety Through Faith*

Lorraine Murray's honesty, gentleness, understanding,
and compassion reach out from every page of this
book. She helps us remember that we are not alone, that
God is with us, and that there is comfort to be found
even in the darkest circumstances. Whether you have
recently received word of a life-changing diagnosis, or
you are facing other trials in your life, Murray's honest,
open, storytelling style will shine a light on your own
experiences and help you see your trials in a new,
healing way.

KATHERINE MURRAY
author of more than fifty books, and
publisher of "Practical Faith," an online
journal sharing simple stories of daily faith

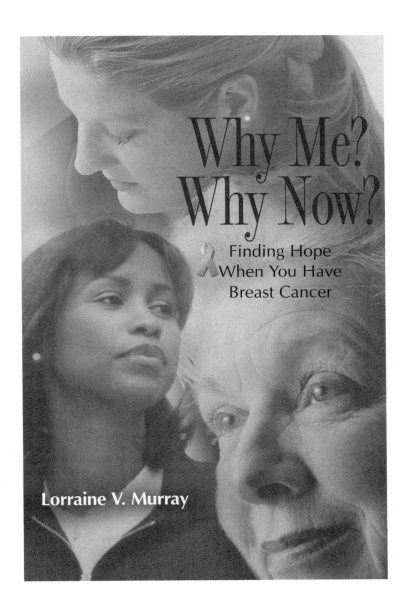

Why Me?
Why Now?

Finding Hope
When You Have
Breast Cancer

Lorraine V. Murray

ave maria press Notre Dame, Indiana

---

www.avemariapress.com

International Standard Book Number: 0-87793-992-6

Cover and text design by Katherine Robinson Coleman

Printed and bound in the United States of America.

Library of Congress Cataloging-in-Publication Data

Murray, Lorraine.
  Why me? why now? : finding hope when you have breast cancer / Lorraine Murray.
     p. cm.
Includes bibliographical references.
  ISBN 0-87793-992-6 (pbk.)
  1. Breast cancer—Patients—Religious life. 2. Breast cancer—Religious aspects—Christianity. 3. Murray, Lorraine. I.
Title.

  BV4910.33.M87 2003
  248.8'619699449—dc21

                                                          2003007350

To my sisters,
Rosemary, Lisa,
Pam, and Barbara,

And my second
mom, Lou.

"The people who
walked in darkness
have seen a great light."

—Isaiah 9:2

Contents

Acknowledgments

*T*his book would not have taken shape without generous outpourings of kindness and prayers from so many people who helped me through the darkest time of my life.

I am deeply grateful to my beloved husband, Jef, and my dearest friend, Pam Mottram, who have helped me feel God's love time and again, through hugs, encouraging words, and their deep compassion; and to the beloved Murray clan, who have been true family to me from day one.

I extend heartfelt thanks to the priests whose prayers and loving counsel have calmed my fears, especially Monsignor Richard Lopez, my spiritual director; Fr. Frank X. Richardson, pastor at St. Thomas More Church; and Fr. Pavol Brenkus, parochial vicar at St. Thomas More Church.

I am blessed with wonderful doctors, especially Dr. Grattan C. Woodson, III; Dr. John S. Kennedy, who performed the surgery; Dr. David Holladay, who supervised the radiation therapy; and Dr. Richard Stiles, the radiologist at St. Joseph's Hospital in Atlanta who first detected the problem on my x-rays.

A big hug goes to Daniel W. Driscoll, my editor at Ave Maria Press, who graciously shepherded my manuscript from start to finish—and another hug to Maureen Walsh, who led me to him.

My gratitude extends to other editors who have nurtured my writing efforts, especially Diane Lore and Ron Friedman at the *Atlanta Journal-Constitution*; Fr. Thomas Reese, S.J., and Fr. Francis Turnbull, S.J., at *America* magazine; Gretchen Keiser and Rebecca Rakoczy at the *Georgia Bulletin*; and Katherine Bruss and Kate Egan at the American Cancer Society.

My prayers of thanksgiving also embrace my Aunt Rita and Uncle Ray; the Mende and Metcalf clans; the Mottrams and the McNeeses; the Andersons and the Rosascos; Claire and Tom; Margaret Lee and Patty; Sues and Jeff; and Janie and Kevin.

I am thankful for Pat Graham and my colleagues in the Pitts Theology Library at Emory University, for welcoming me so warmly into their midst when I was still reeling from the shock of my diagnosis, and for encouraging my writing efforts.

And I wish blessings upon all the folks who kept me smiling, even during the roughest times, especially my mother-in-law, Lou; my sister, Rosemary; my nieces, Chrissy and Jenifer; my goddaughter, Sarah, and her brother, Stephen; my confirmation goddaughter, Katie; and the choir and my faith community at St. Thomas More Church.

Amen.

Introduction

He came and took her by the hand
and lifted her up.

—Mark 1:31 [NRSV]

*I*t happened over three years ago, but still
there are times when I find myself reeling
in disbelief. "It can't be possible," I sigh.
"This can't have happened to me." But the truth is
that it did happen to me.

I was one of the high-risk women, and still the
breast cancer diagnosis on May 18, 2000, hit me
like a tidal wave. For many years, I'd ticked off the
risk factors for breast cancer on a mental checklist,
fretting about how many I had. No kids, that was
one tick. A mom who'd died from the disease. Tick.
Early onset of menstruation and late onset of
menopause. Tick, tick.

Still, I had reassured myself that I was fending off
the illness by my fierce commitment to health,
which had blossomed right after my mom's death

11

when I was twenty-nine. No red meat for me. No white bread either. Instead, plenty of high-fiber foods and fresh vegetables. When I read that soy was supposed to be a protection against breast cancer, I talked myself into liking tofu and soy milk. I took vitamins. I walked two to three miles a day. I went for checkups and began having yearly mammograms at age forty, as the doctors had advised. I thought that I'd devised a magical formula for avoiding my worst nightmare, but how wrong I was.

If I've learned anything from my cancer diagnosis, it's that the illusion of control over our lives is just that—an illusion. This is not to say we should pull out all the stops, gain one hundred pounds, and take up smoking. But it's important to acknowledge that we are not in the driver's seat. Someone Else is steering the big car of life and planning our itinerary, while we are the ones sitting in the back seat. As backseat drivers, we can certainly make our desires known, but we're not ultimately responsible for the outcome of the trip.

When the surgeon telephoned to tell me the results of the biopsy, I felt myself sinking into a vast ocean of fear. Looking back now, after more than three years have passed, I marvel that I managed to swim safely to shore. I believe that I've been kept afloat by prayer, scriptural reflections, and the endlessly kind gestures of family and friends. Along the way, I have discovered some spiritual insights that have kept me reasonably sane, and my hope is that these insights will help you too.

First, a little about me. I was born into an Italian-American, Roman Catholic family, attended

Catholic schools until I was eighteen, and then became a "fallen away" Catholic when I went to college and bagged a graduate degree in philosophy. Years later, when I was in my forties, I returned to the church, and I have never regretted going back. Even though I am somewhat untraditional in my approach to Catholicism, and sometimes grumble over my disagreements with the powers that be, I'm committed to following Jesus Christ, and for me, Catholicism is the best path. The rituals, the prayers, and the beliefs of this ancient religion are in my blood, and they suit me well. Still, I must emphasize that I've written this book for women of *all* Christian faiths and backgrounds.

When I decided to write a book about cancer, at first I thought I would sidestep spiritual issues and simply present one-size-fits-all advice for women struggling emotionally after their cancer diagnoses. Before long, however, I realized that I couldn't write from the heart about my illness without grounding my statements in my Christian faith. To advise you on navigating your way safely through this illness without mentioning prayer and scripture would be like handing you a recipe for a hot fudge sundae that lacked chocolate, the most vital ingredient.

I have no doubt that I could not have arrived at the place I am today without a ton of prayers, a bushel of scriptural reading, spiritual guidance, numerous conversations with God, and generous doses of his sweet and generous grace.

Early in my illness, I had a strong feeling that I should start working on a book about faith and cancer, but I kept avoiding the project. Somehow I feared that if I attempted to write a book on cancer, I would be forced to confront daily, for months at a time, the details of my illness and I would never leave the illness behind me and get on with my life. Gradually, though, I came to see that, unless I wrote this book, I would never get on with my life. I've come to see that writing this book is a part of my life, just as my illness is. Running away can do no good. Facing cancer head-on, and writing about it, has become my way of ministering to other women on the same path.

Since writing comes so naturally to me and is a gift from God, I feel that the book you hold in your hands is my way to share my gift with you. I believe that when we follow our calling and use the gifts God has given us, there are certain clear signs, like renewed energy and joy, which I've felt while writing this book.

This book is divided into three parts that move logically from diagnosis to treatment, and then to recovery. I believe you will find the parts helpful even if you are far beyond the initial stages of diagnosis and treatment. Even if your diagnosis was five or ten years ago, I think that you, and your caregivers as well, will find many helpful insights and suggestions in all three parts. I hope this little book will find its way to church-based groups of Christian women with cancer. If your church doesn't have such a group, please think about starting one. Sometimes all it takes is putting a notice in the church bulletin. If you don't want to be the group leader, just ask for a volunteer at the first session. God has a way of sending the right person to do the job.

I wrote this book to help promote your spiritual and emotional healing, but I also had a selfish reason. I've discovered that as I've faced my fears and doubts and wrangled with the big issues ("Why me? Why now?"), I've also started healing spiritually myself.

There are no easy answers to why a woman gets breast cancer and there is no easy way to recover emotionally after the diagnosis. Recovery can be a rocky road, and if you're like me, you may trip over numerous pebbles—and even a few boulders. I have discovered, however, that whenever you trip, someone will be there to help you up. It may be a sweetheart, a spouse, a parent, a sister, a friend, a minister or a priest—but someone will be there. I have fallen numerous times, and I have been blessed by a stream of people extending their hands. And now it is my turn. This book is my way of helping you up.

Part One

"Why Me? Why Now?":

The Darkness
of the Diagnosis

Surely God is my salvation; I will trust,
and will not be afraid, for the
LORD GOD is my strength and my
might; he has become my salvation.

—Isaiah 12:2 (NRSV)

I will always remember the way my heart
jumped when the phone rang on the
morning of May 18, 2000. I had called
the surgeon's office earlier that morning to get the
results of the biopsy that he had performed on my
breast, and I expected his nurse to call me back

with good news. I remember how I began trembling when I heard the doctor's voice on the line. Although he tried to break the news as gently and compassionately as possible, his words, "There are some cancer cells in there," shook me to my very core. As I collapsed on the couch in tears, I knew my life had changed forever. Although I never said, "Why Me? Why Now?" aloud, these words raged through my mind countless times after his phone call and became the emblems of my suffering.

My first impulse, after bursting into tears, was to call Pam, my best friend, who lives just a few miles away. "I'm on my way," she said, without a moment's hesitation. While I waited for her, I called my mother-in-law, Lou, who lives over seventy miles away, and I was deeply touched when she said, "Do you need company?" Moments later, the phone rang again. The first call was from my sister-in-law, Lisa, and the next one from Steve, my brother-in-law. Although I didn't realize it at the time, their sweet and loving voices on the phone were the first, very precious, signs of the support that God would continue sending me throughout the dark months that lay ahead.

My husband, Jef, was attending an out-of-town business meeting that morning. The surgeon's office had told us that the results of my biopsy would be ready that afternoon, and Jef had planned to be home when I called. But I had felt so antsy that morning that I'd decided to call the surgeon's office on the off chance that the results might be available. I hoped the news would be good, so I could stop fretting and get on with my day. When the news was anything but good, I left a frantic message for Jef at his office, and he rushed home shortly after.

Pam showed up minutes after I called her, carrying her daughter, Sarah—my beloved goddaughter—who was two years old at the time. I didn't want to frighten little Sarah, so when Pam embraced me, I tried to stem the giant storm of tears that was threatening to overtake me. As she held me, Pam said something that returned to my mind, time and again, during the next few months. "This is not the same thing that happened to your mother," she said gently.

I desperately needed to hear those words, because cancer and death had been synonymous in my mother's journey. She had been diagnosed with breast cancer in 1972 and had died in 1976, at the age of sixty-four. Like most daughters of women who have died of the disease, I was well aware that I was in a high-risk category and I had dreaded my yearly mammograms.

As you read this book, I encourage you to keep Pam's words in mind. Although the word "cancer" may strike terror into your heart, there are many avenues of treatment today that didn't exist in our mothers' day. Surgery, radiation and chemotherapy, and new drugs help women with breast cancer today live healthy lives long after the initial shock of the diagnosis has worn off. Cancer may be a frightening, life-changing event, but it is not a death sentence.

Now that over three years have passed since my diagnosis, I can say with all honesty that I've learned more about myself during this time than I ever dreamed imaginable. Although I would not recommend a cancer diagnosis as a way to arrive at self-knowledge, facing an illness of this kind changes you forever. At first, you may think all the changes are negative. I was concerned that I had lost my peace of mind and would never get it back. I worried that the day would never come when I would climb out of bed in the morning without "why me, why now?" as the first thought that popped into my mind.

As the months have passed, however, I believe I have experienced positive changes and many outpourings of God's grace from facing cancer. Looking back, I can detect spiritual insights that carried me through the dark months following the shock of the diagnosis. Even on the bleakest days, there were glimpses of Christ's loving light. And I feel blessed to share these little illuminations with you in Part One of this book.

One

The Lesson of Mary and Martha

He heals the brokenhearted,
and binds up their wounds.

—Psalm 147:3 (NRSV)

*I*n the weeks following my cancer
diagnosis, I began abandoning my usual
routines. Although I'd always been strict
about keeping an orderly house, I found myself
allowing stacks of magazines and books to pile up.
Dust bunnies moseyed across the floor, and I felt
no impulse to banish them. Looking back now, I
see that I was learning an important lesson about
life. It is OK to let go of some things. You don't
have to be Ms. Perfect. People who really love you

23

will not criticize you if your house is not in apple-pie order and your yard isn't a scene out of *Home Beautiful.*

The Better Part

There is a wonderful story in the New Testament about Jesus' visit to Mary and Martha, who were sisters. While Martha busied herself in the kitchen, fretting over the details of domestic life, as we all do at times, Mary sat calmly by Jesus' feet, gazing lovingly into his eyes. Martha was feeling burdened by all her work and she went to Jesus and said, "Lord, do you not care that my sister has left me by myself to do the serving? Tell her to help me." But Jesus didn't turn to Mary and command that she help her sister. Instead, he replied, "Martha, Martha, you are anxious and worried about many things" (Lk 10:40, 41).

Those words really spoke to me when I was newly diagnosed. It seemed that "anxious and worried about many things" could have been the slogan on my cancer T-shirt. It helped me to see that Jesus understood Martha, who felt so burdened by her responsibilities. He treated her very gently. He didn't condemn her or chastise her. Instead, he told her, "There is need of only one thing."

What is that one thing? What is the one necessary thing that Jesus expects from all of us? He explained: "Mary has chosen the better part and it will not be taken from her" (Lk 10:42). His words speak to all Christians, with special meaning for women with breast cancer. The words show us that we have a choice. We can choose to feel burdened, anxious, and worried, and run around in a panic, or we can make a real effort to react otherwise. What did Mary do? She "sat beside the Lord at his feet listening to him speak." She chose Jesus.

There are two parts of the lesson. First, we must take time from our busy and anxious lives to spend time with God, however we can. Maybe that means going to church to pray, or maybe it means praying in our garden, or taking a long walk and feeling God's presence. The second part of the lesson is that unless we carve out some space for God, we may never hear his voice. What did Jesus say to Mary? The gospel writers do not tell us, but he evidently had special messages just for her, and he has special words for us too.

Maybe we can't be like Mary all the time, spending hours sitting at the feet of Jesus and contemplating him, but how often do we let a whole day pass without giving him a moment's thought?

Our days overflow with duties and chores, but cancer has a way of making us sit up and wonder what is really important. I have come to see that there is no cosmic rule book that states that you must have matching curtains and wallpaper, or a gleaming bathroom floor. Some days, especially while you are still experiencing the initial shock waves of your diagnosis, you may not feel like making the bed or tidying up the living room. If you find it hard to give yourself permission to be sloppy once in a while, then, please, let me have the honor. Here is your permission: It is OK to be sloppy now and again. It is OK to let some things go. God still loves you.

No Strings Attached

Even if you fail to emulate the ladies that grace the pages of the glossy magazines, those superwomen of domestic bliss, God still loves you. Keep in mind that Jesus loved people with no strings attached. "Now Jesus loved Martha and her sister and Lazarus," John tells us (Jn 11:5). Jesus' heart was so big that he loved Martha and Mary both, even if Martha was busy and anxious and didn't take the time to sit at his feet.

Jesus didn't tell the lepers that he would heal them *if* they tithed. He didn't tell the thief on the cross that he would forgive the man his sins *if* the man recited the proper prayers. Jesus loved people as they were, in their sinfulness, their drunkenness, their illnesses, their doubts, their despair—and their messiness. He loves you the same way, with no strings attached, and he will still love you if your life slips into chaos for a while.

"God's love for us does not depend on what we do or say, on our looks or intelligence, on our success or popularity," wrote Henri Nouwen in *Bread for the Journey*. "God's love for us existed before we were born and will exist after we have died."

Tending to the Little Ones

If you are a mom, you have to keep the home ship afloat for your little ones. They will expect the same bowls of oatmeal in the morning and the same freshly laundered clothes that you so lovingly provided before your diagnosis. But when you are in crisis mode, your energy may dwindle, so it's essential to set priorities and keep them. If you have a choice between scrubbing the bathroom tiles or reading a story to your toddler, tell the tiles they can wait. And if you are feeling overwhelmed, ask friends or family members to help you. When people hear about a cancer diagnosis, the first question they usually ask is: "What can I do?" It helps to have a specific answer. You may want to ask an aunt to come watch the kids one day a week or let the kids stay over at grandma's house on the weekend to give you a break.

Who Cares?

Before my diagnosis, I was one of those nitpicking housekeepers who had to damp mop the floors if guests were coming for dinner. In the months following the diagnosis, however, I loosened up a little. It is immensely cathartic to say "Who cares?" at least once a day. You didn't floss your teeth tonight. So who cares? And will the world end if you don't sweep the front porch? One day, I made a sign out of construction paper and taped it to my fridge. It proclaimed: "This place was condemned by Martha Stewart." I felt better after that.

I also stopped apologizing to friends about the stacks of magazines and books in the living room, and I didn't feel mortified if someone used the bathroom before I'd had a chance to scour the sink. I tend to be very critical of myself—and my surroundings—and it was hard to stop being so demanding, but I didn't feel I had a choice. I was so overwhelmed emotionally by the diagnosis that I really didn't have the energy to sweep and scrub and dust. It took every ounce of my energy to get out of bed, dress myself, and comb my hair. I gave myself extra bonus points if I also managed to dab on some lipstick.

Time Is Precious

Now that three years have passed, and my energy has fully returned, I admit that I have resumed my search-and-destroy mission against dust bunnies, but if a friend calls to invite me out for coffee, I drop the mop and head for the door. If cancer teaches you anything about life, it is this: Time is precious. All of us, cancer survivors or not, have a limited amount of hours, minutes, and seconds left on Planet Earth. Let's enjoy them.

Let's stop criticizing ourselves. Let's stop being so busy. Let's remind ourselves, over and over, that God loves us, even when our homes look like Martha Stewart's nightmare. And instead of rushing around like Martha in the New Testament, let's spend some prayerful time imitating her sister, Mary. Let's remember to choose "the better part." Instead of bustling around, getting overwhelmed by the details of our lives, and falling into a panic about our illness, let's sit at the feet of Jesus. He speaks to us in our joys and celebrations, and in our sorrows and pains. He speaks to us even in cancer. Let's listen to him.

Prayer

Heavenly Father, you know every inch of my heart. I realize my life is in your big hands, but at times I forget, and I find myself so afraid and worried. Help me, God, to get through the shock of this gigantic change in my life. Help me to realize there are excellent treatments for this disease. Let me be thankful to the person who discovered the cancer. Let me be grateful to my friends and family who are here to help me. Help me, God, to see that there will be light in this darkness. Help me to see your hand in my illness. Give me the grace to see that it is all right to let go of some things in my life now. Let me take to heart the lesson of Mary and Martha. Give me the grace to choose the better part. I pray in Jesus' name. Amen.

Scriptural Reflections and Questions for Discussion

Again and again in scripture, God sends us messages to let us know him better and to convey his tender feelings for us. Especially in times of illness, it helps to be aware of God's many loving and comforting words in the Bible. As you read scripture, make the scene personal. Put yourself into the story and keep in mind that God is talking to you.

1. Read Psalm 118:1–4, Psalm 103:1–5, and Matthew 9:36. What is God telling you about himself?

2. Read Matthew 11:28–30. What is Jesus promising you?

3. Read Mark 1:31, Mark 5:41, and Mark 9:27. Imagine that you are the person with

Jesus in each story and then reflect on the following question: How is Jesus lifting you up during your illness?

4. When are you most like Mary? When do you feel like Martha?

Exercise 1

Write a prayer expressing your feelings about your illness to God.

Exercise 2

Make a list entitled "Who Cares?" enumerating some responsibilities at work and at home that you can let go of.

Two

"Oh, God, Help Me!"

Then he said to them:
"I am deeply grieved, even to death."

—Matthew 26:38a (NRSV)

J am usually rather placid and quiet as I pray, but there was a day, not long after that phone call from the surgeon, when I found myself actually shouting at God. I was trying to decide what kind of surgery to have. The surgeon, whom I trusted and respected, had recommended a lumpectomy, but another doctor, whom I'd known for many years, had suggested a mastectomy. Even though the surgeon had assured me that I didn't have to make my decision overnight, I felt I couldn't waffle forever.

I was home alone one afternoon, sitting on the couch. To be more precise, I was weeping on the couch. Should I chose the more conservative plan or the more radical plan? I had friends who'd had lumpectomies and were pleased with the results, but I also knew other women who said a mastectomy was the best plan.

Shouting at God

Suddenly I was seized with anger. How in the world had I gotten myself into this predicament? How was I going to extricate myself? Was I going to die of this stinking, miserable, horrible disease just like my mother had? And how was I going to make my decision? I am a notoriously wishy-washy person, someone who anguishes over tiny matters, like where to eat lunch or what blouse to wear, things that other people decide in a heartbeat. Suddenly I found myself weeping and shouting at God. "WHAT DO YOU WANT ME TO DO? WHAT AM I SUPPOSED TO DO? TELL ME, TELL ME! HELP ME, HELP ME, I'M SO SCARED, I'M SO SCARED. OH, GOD, HELP ME!"

Mysterious Ways

I cried until my eyes were nearly swollen shut and I was exhausted. I still hadn't made my decision, but I was seized by a raging desire for a treat. When the image of a nearby health food store flashed in my mind, I knew what the immediate plan would be. I'd wash my face and comb my hair and head to the health food store for ice cream. When I arrived at the store, I took a different route than I usually did and ended up in the book section. As I gazed at the shelves through swollen eyes, one book seemed to light up. It was by a well-respected surgeon, detailing the pros and cons of various therapies and treatments for breast cancer. What a coincidence, I thought. Then I remembered that God works in mysterious ways and everything is part of his plan, and nothing is really accidental.

I ate the ice cream, bought the book, and headed home. The next day, after I'd read a good portion of the book, my prayers were answered. I felt I had found the necessary factual information I needed to make my decision. And when my husband came home and I told him about my decision to have the lumpectomy, I felt a sense of peace.

Putting on Spiritual Makeup

Sometimes we forget that God loves us, no matter what our emotional state might be. We think we have to put on spiritual makeup before we can talk to him. After all, we spruce ourselves up before going to church, so surely we also should "put on our faces" every time we pray. That afternoon, though, I dropped all the pretenses and threw myself at God just as I was—unadorned, suffering, and desperate. And I learned a lesson. I realized that God loves us when we're mad at him, and he loves us when we snub him. God loves us when we shout at him in desperation, and he loves us when we are sad and lonely. Like a mother, God just loves us, no matter what.

As you pray about your decisions, don't worry about saying the right prayers or lighting the candles in exactly the right way. Just pray. The words will arise to your lips spontaneously—and he will answer you. Sometimes he answers you through books, sometimes through other people. It may take a little time, but you'll know when you have the right answer.

Jesus in the Garden

When I was in a state of great emotional turmoil, it helped me to remember that when Jesus prayed in the Garden of Gethsemane on the night before his death, he prayed in an impassioned, fiery way. "He was in such agony and he prayed so fervently that his sweat became like drops of blood falling on the ground" (Lk 22:44). If we really dwell on that image in our hearts, we can feel closer to Jesus in our own agony over cancer. Mark tells us that Jesus was "troubled and distressed" (14:33). These words suited me to a tee during the early days of my diagnosis. It helped me to remember that Jesus did not separate himself from the sorrows and agonies of human experience. We are not alone in our emotional distress.

When Jesus prayed in the garden, he didn't use the carefully prescribed prayers that the Jews of the time followed when they prayed in the Temple. There were prayers for every occasion, and there were rituals for all the big moments of life, and Jesus knew them all. But on the night before he died, he did not go to the Temple to pray, nor did he use any standard prayers. Instead, he presented himself to the Father just as he was: trembling and sweating and agonizing.

After you have prayed and decided on your course of treatment, don't look back. Don't second-guess yourself or wonder if you did the right thing. Don't torture yourself with "what ifs" as in: "What if I'd had the other procedure?" or "What if I'd gone to a different doctor?" Remember Lot's wife in the Old Testament? She was warned not to look back or she'd turn into stone. I believe the story of Lot's wife is a warning against fretting over the past, which is over and done with. God is directing our decisions, even if we aren't aware of his presence. Pray for the faith that believes everything that happens is part of God's plan for us.

Prayer

Lord: Sometimes I am so filled with grief over my illness and so shocked that it happened to me. I feel like a river of tears is pouring from my eyes. I feel like I am in the Garden of Gethsemane, sorrowful and troubled. But I know, deep inside, that you will dry every tear and come to my rescue. I know that you are with me in sorrow and in joy. You are there in the storm and in the calm. You reveal your loving presence in doctors and nurses and in the tender concern of my family and friends. There are times I am so weary and brokenhearted, but you always lift me up. I praise you and I love you. Amen.

Scriptural Reflections and Questions for Discussion

The psalms describe the whole realm of human emotions, ranging from grief and anger to delight and joy. They show us that God will listen when we speak to him from the depths of our hearts, and God will never desert us, even when we feel close to despair.

1. Read Psalm 6 and Psalm 86:1–7. What are some emotions that the psalmist is expressing? Do any of these speak to your heart?

2. Read Psalm 34:5–7. How is God delivering you from your fears?

3. Read Isaiah 61:1–3 and Isaiah 66:13. What is God's promise to you?

Exercise 1

Write a prayer to God asking for physical, emotional, and spiritual healing.

Exercise 2

Imagine you are with Jesus in the Garden of Gethsemane, where he is praying to let the cup pass him by. Describe your "cup" to Jesus as it relates to breast cancer.

Three

I Didn't Realize
My Friends Had Wings

Some have entertained
angels without knowing it.

—Hebrews 13:2 (NRSV)

On the night before the crucifixion, when Jesus went to the garden with his friends to pray, he told them, "My soul is sorrowful even to death" (Mk 14:34). He then fell to the ground and prayed to the Father, who heard his anguished cries for help and sent him an angel to give him strength.

God sends angels to women with breast cancer to help us weather the storm of our illness. But these angels aren't clothed in snowy garments or adorned with sparkling halos. Instead, they are very ordinary people, sometimes seated across from us at the breakfast table, speaking from the pulpit on Sunday, or living in the house next door. If you start keeping an eye out for them, I assure you that you will see them everywhere.

Is This Heaven?

On the day of my surgery, my angels were definitely by my side. My husband, Jef, took me to the hospital, where my best friend, Pam, my sister-in-law, Lisa, and my mother-in-law, Lou, joined us. Just before the nurse wheeled me into surgery, each of my angels bent down to give me a kiss. When I awoke in the recovery room, the first words from my lips were, "Is this heaven?" The sweet and kind nurses who were tending to me answered gently that it wasn't, but I think my question arose from my heart because I felt so cherished. I really felt that I was in the presence of angels.

There have been many more angels in my life since that day. Some are people I've never met, folks who read my articles in the *Atlanta Journal-Constitution* or in *America* magazine and send me uplifting e-mails or letters brimming with prayers and love. During the early days of my diagnosis, and then after surgery, my out-of-town family members also showed their love by telephoning often. Just hearing the voices of my sister, Rosemary, my nieces, Jenifer and Chrissy, my cousin Julie, and my Aunt Rita lifted my spirits enormously.

I was surprised to discover another angel when I was in my own private Garden of Gethsemane, and he was my surgeon. When I first met Dr. John S. Kennedy, I was in a state of great anguish. I was so overwhelmed with fear and anxiety that I had trouble understanding many of his explanations about treatments and prognoses. I was grateful that Jef came with me and took copious notes, which he explained to me later. Still, despite my emotional distress, I remember that I felt an instant kinship with Dr. Kennedy, whose gentle and kind demeanor impressed me. He was also very calm, which was a great gift to someone in turmoil.

Praying Before Surgery

Once the date was set for the surgery, I felt an impulse to ask Dr. Kennedy to pray with me. I don't know where the impulse came from, but it was very strong, and I wondered if God was sending me a message. I was a little hesitant, however, because in my past experience, medicine and faith hadn't seemed to mix. Most of the doctors I had seen over the years had treated my body with very little discussion of my soul. Physical and spiritual concerns had been kept in separate compartments.

I noticed a bible in Dr. Kennedy's waiting room, and I took this to be an encouraging sign. One day, I decided to run the idea of praying by his nurse. "Do you think the doctor might pray with me before surgery?" I asked. Her face lit up, and she assured me that the doctor and his family were "very devout Christians." She felt confident that he would not turn me down. Shortly after, during another appointment, I mustered up the courage to ask him, and he agreed without a moment's hesitation.

On the day of my surgery, I was lying in the operating room, just beginning to get woozy from the anesthesia, when he walked in and took my hand. The last memory I have before falling asleep is the two of us saying the Lord's Prayer together. Dr. Kennedy prayed some of the words of the prayer a little differently than I did. He said "debts" instead of "trespasses," for example. However, the differences didn't matter at all, and I remember feeling a little sense of pride that I managed to get all the way to the "Amen" before blacking out.

The surgery was performed on an outpatient basis, so once I was able to get dressed and wobble into the car, Jef drove me home. As soon as I got into the house, I climbed groggily into bed, while he went to fill a prescription for pain relievers at the drugstore, and my friend Pam kept watch over me. Although I had mentally braced myself for an onslaught of pain, I never took the medication. I was surprised to discover that a few aspirin were all I needed to handle the soreness.

The morning after surgery, I climbed gingerly out of bed, expecting to feel absolutely terrible, and although I was very weak, I had enough strength to have breakfast in the dining room and then walk into the yard to check my roses. I remembered all the people who had assured me of prayers, and in that moment, I had a sense that all these angels were somehow lifting me up and sustaining me with their faith.

Hugs

In the weeks to come, I regained my strength. I ate well, got plenty of sleep, and remembered to get exercise every day. All these things helped me, but I feel that the companionship and love that flowed from my friends were the main ingredients in my recovery. Hugs were such a big help, especially on the days when I felt like a teddy bear coming apart at the seams. Every time someone gave me a big hug, I felt a surge of joy and energy that blocked out all my anxiety.

On the days when you are feeling downtrodden or anxious, try this little experiment. Go up to your sweetheart, your husband, or a good friend and stretch out your arms for a hug. I'm not talking about a quick embrace in which you barely touch the other person. I mean the kind of hug that seems to dissolve the boundaries between you both. It's not always easy to ask for a hug, but I have discovered that the angels in your life won't turn you down.

Signs of Peace

One of my favorite parts of the Mass is when the priest encourages the congregation to "offer each other a sign of Christ's peace." Many people shake hands and smile, but the signs of peace that I really enjoy are huge hugs from Pam and Jef. The other day after Mass, I looked down and saw my goddaughter, Sarah, wrapping her arms around my knees in a fervent embrace. When I reached down to return her hug, my purse slipped off my shoulder. "Oh, I hugged you too tight," the child said. But I quickly assured this little angel, "Honey, don't worry. You can't ever hug too tight!"

Food

In addition to providing hugs, you may discover that the angels in your life come bearing gifts of food. Upon my return from the hospital on the day of my surgery, I was pleasantly surprised to discover that my special angels had laden our front porch with little love offerings of food. Friends originally from Louisiana had delivered a pot of crawfish stew. Another friend, Margaret, who is an expert baker, left some delicious bread. There were also boxes of chocolates and platters of cookies.

Sharing the Pain

My experience with cancer has shown me, over and over, how important my loved ones are to me. Looking back, I cannot see how I could have survived without their visits, gifts, cards, phone calls, and e-mails. Jesus told his friends that when two or three gathered in his name, he would make his presence known. He has certainly made his presence known in my life through the endless kindnesses of my friends. Christianity doesn't work in a vacuum. We can pray alone, but we can't love or serve without the presence of others. I think that's why, when Jesus taught the disciples how to pray, he didn't say, "*My* father, who art in heaven," and he didn't say, "Give *me* this day *my* daily bread." Instead, he shaped the prayer using the plural, which reveals to us the importance of community.

Women with cancer need a community of loving and compassionate people to help us heal emotionally, physically, and spiritually. We can take our cue from Jesus in the Garden of Gethsemane, when he turned to his friends and asked for their prayers. We can also remember that he had someone to help him carry the weight of his cross as he walked to Golgotha. There is no shame in admitting we need the helping hands, friendly faces, or the open hearts of others.

Alcoholics Anonymous has a wonderful motto, "Pain shared is pain halved," which I think speaks to women with cancer. It is true that suffering is lessened when you share your woes with another person. Some days you may feel like a prisoner within your own mind, tormented by worries and fears. The longer you hold the anguish inside, the more it seems to build. Try telling a friend, "I'm having a bad day. I feel like I'm sinking," and almost immediately the shadow starts to recede. Something mysterious and wonderful happens when you share your worries with someone else. As you feel the negative energy being released from your soul, you begin to tap into the wonderful healing power of another's love.

About a week after learning that I had cancer, I attended a women's cancer support group at a local hospital. The first night I arrived at the hospital, my eyes were nearly swollen shut from crying, and I could barely see. I was in a state of pure panic. The other women, including some who had been attending the support group for years, were incredibly kind and nurturing. They allowed me to weep and tell my story and told me about their own journeys. They reassured me. And, most important, they gave me hugs all around.

I went to the group a few more times, but then dropped out when I started the seven weeks of radiation therapy. Problem was, I was dealing with so many fears that listening to some of the women's stories made me more anxious. Later, I attended a few meetings of another cancer support group, and then, after radiation therapy, I tried a third group. But my attendance in these groups was short-lived. It took me a while to realize that the kind of support I was seeking was spiritual, and the support groups were secular. I didn't feel I could talk openly about the role of my Christian faith in my cancer journey with others who might not share my beliefs.

Although I didn't realize it at the time, I believe God was calling me to launch the kind of group I was seeking, which was a Christian support group for women with cancer, where women could explore the spiritual aspects of their journeys. It was only after I was in the recovery phase of my illness that I heeded the call and started a spiritual support group at my church.

Still, support groups aren't for everyone. Some women get the help they need from confiding in a spouse, a sweetheart, a sister, or a friend. Other women, however, really feel the need to talk with other cancer survivors. If you don't feel you have the support group you need, you may want to consider launching a group at your church, seeking spiritual counseling, or finding a spiritual director.

Many women start attending support groups seeking help for themselves, but stay in the group to offer support to others. The sharing of pain is a two-way street, and just as many of the folks in Alcoholics Anonymous have been "dry" for years, many women in cancer support groups have long been cancer-free, but they are there to be angels to others.

Prayer

God, I thank you for the angels you have sent to help me on my journey. You know, dear One, that when it seems that my heart is breaking, a friend will suddenly telephone or stop by to give me a hug or share a meal, and suddenly I feel lifted up again. Help me, my beloved Jesus, to recognize angels everywhere, especially in the medical community, where so many give of themselves so compassionately. Help me also to recognize people in my life who might need a kind word, a kiss, or some other sign of affection. Help me to become an angel to others. Amen.

Scriptural Reflections and Questions for Discussion

1. Read Luke 23:26. Who are the people in your life who are helping you bear the cross of your illness?

2. Read Psalm 40:2–4. How has the Lord heard your cry in the past? How has he steadied you?

3. Read Jesus' question in John 20:15. What would your answer be? Why are you weeping?

Exercise 1

During the upcoming week, perform a simple experiment. Hug at least one person a day. Journal your findings.

Exercise 2

Write a prayer thanking God for the angels in your life.

Part Two

Glimpsing Light at the End of the Tunnel: Treatment

"Come to me, all you who labor and are burdened, and I will give you rest."

—Matthew 11:28

I dedicate this section of the book to any reader who has found herself, box of Kleenex in hand, sitting on the couch, wearing a scraggly bathrobe and fuzzy slippers, and wondering if she has the energy to get dressed. I dedicate it to any woman who has looked in the mirror at eyes swollen from weeping and wondered whether makeup could work a miracle, and to any woman who has at times felt paralyzed by a steady stream of "what ifs."

When I learned that I would need seven weeks of radiation therapy treatments, I was stunned. That seemed like an eternity. I pictured myself dragging around, bone-weary and nauseated, for seven weeks. The only bright piece of news was that there is an excellent, highly touted radiation therapy clinic located only ten minutes from my home. I found it interesting that I had passed this place so many times before and had never given any thought to all the people who were streaming in the doors in search of treatment.

On the day I reported for the first radiation treatment, I was a nervous wreck. Even though the doctors had assured me that I wouldn't feel a thing during radiation therapy, on some deep level I didn't believe them. I expected pain.

It didn't take me long to conclude, though, that I had to surrender my doubts and walk forward in faith. I don't have a medical degree, but the radiologists and other doctors treating me did, and there was no sense in doubting them. And so I tried to be as cheerful as I could as I took my place on an examining table, lying flat on my back, while the technician, a young woman I had never met before, tattooed a tiny black dot between my breasts. That tiny dot was hugely important, I discovered later, since the other technicians used it to position the equipment that delivered the radiation beam.

During my next few visits, I discovered that the doctors had been correct. Radiation therapy didn't hurt at all. The machine that I had to lie under was daunting, but I didn't feel any sensations during the time I was positioned under the big beam. Since it took the technicians a few minutes to position my breast exactly right, I used that time to utter a mental prayer. "God, I don't understand how any of this works. It's really beyond me. The beam is invisible. I trust that the technicians have me in the right position and the beam is doing its job. I put myself totally in your hands. May the light of radiation heal my breast, and may your light heal my heart."

I was very fortunate. I experienced no nausea or other side effects, other than a little fatigue. I took extra naps and also made an effort to get nine to ten hours of sleep a night while trying to keep up with my other routines like taking walks with my husband (and complaining of the distance a little more than usual!).

Still, I was struggling with my fears of the unknown, and it was hard to turn off my worry machine. I had been raised to believe that one should avoid radiation at all costs, but now I was subjecting my body to seven weeks' worth of nearly daily doses. I understood, of course, that the amount of radiation exposure was carefully controlled, but still some deep part of me fretted about the long-term effects. During treatments, I often felt that I'd entered a dark and mysterious tunnel that seemed to stretch on forever. What would I find at the other end?

One of my first chilling thoughts after diagnosis was that I would have to go through chemotherapy. My only knowledge of chemo was somewhat primitive, dating back to 1972, when my poor mom suffered horribly from the side effects, especially nausea. She had also lost every trace of her hair. I have to confess that, despite all my insecurities about my looks (Is my nose too big? Am I too fat? What about those wrinkles?), I am a rather vain person. I have spent my adult life obsessing about my hair. Should I cut it? Curl it? Layer it? Wear it long? Wear it short? Highlight it? Perm it? One thing is for certain: like most women, I had no desire to appear in public without it.

When I first was diagnosed, I prepared myself for the worst. I began trying on scarves one night, and even though I didn't look as fetching as I might have hoped, I decided that if I did lose my hair, scarves would be my fashion statement, rather than wigs or hats. But a few days after surgery, when Jef and I met with Dr. Kennedy, he told us he had good news. The tumor had been discovered very early and had been very small, so chemotherapy would not be necessary.

I was thrilled to avoid chemo, but my heart went out to the women I saw at the radiation therapy center who had not been so fortunate. Many, I noticed sadly, had lost their hair. But after my first waves of pity subsided, I began taking a closer look and soon noticed that all the women seemed to be reacting differently to their predicament. Some women were wearing wigs. Some women were wearing jaunty and upbeat hats, while others had covered their heads with colorful scarves. I was very impressed by the women who had made the choice to do nothing at all to cover up their baldness.

As I saw people at the radiation center from all walks of life suffering from every form of cancer from prostate to throat, I realized that everyone reacts differently to illness—and there is no commandment that says you must handle every aspect of cancer graciously. Some people were very placid, while others seemed emotionally shattered. So if you are facing radiation therapy or chemotherapy and you feel inclined to rant and rave to God about how terrible the situation is, I wouldn't try to stop you. One thing I believe deeply is that God is an excellent listener, and I don't think he minds when his children cry on his shoulder.

The emotions associated with cancer can be very intense, but they are a normal part of the journey. As you undergo treatments for cancer, you may feel like you're creeping through a dark tunnel of fear and worry, but don't despair. Peer into the darkness and you will see glimpses of God's light and grace—and he will help you confront and tame your fears.

Four

Where Is God in My Suffering?

The LORD supports all who
are falling and raises up all
who are bowed down.

—Psalm 145:14

*I*f you were to interview all the women sitting in a doctor's office waiting to hear the results of a test for cancer, I believe you would discover they are all thinking the same thing. "I hope I don't have cancer" or, in other words, "Dear God, let this cup pass from me."

Sadly, millions of women each year are forced to pick up the chalice of suffering as they face the alarming news about their illnesses.

The chalice of suffering passed to me on the day the surgeon called me with the results of my biopsy. I can't say that I picked up the cup very willingly, though. Instead, I fell completely apart. It took me a while to regain my equilibrium enough to begin reading scripture, but when I did, I found comfort in words expressing surrender to God's will.

Let It Be

Mary expressed her surrender to God's will after the angel visited her and told her about the special child she was going to bear. She was astonished and perplexed, and not a little frightened, and she didn't hesitate to voice her concern: "How can this be, since I am a virgin?" But then, instead of surrendering to doubts and fears, Mary acquiesced to God's will with the words, "Let it be with me according to your word" (Lk 1:34, 38 NRSV).

Mary's struggle to accept God's will speaks to the heart of every woman who has ever wondered what God was asking of her. We sometimes forget that Mary had emotions that echo our own. As Gerald Vann points out in *The Pain of Christ and the Sorrow of God*, we are wrong to think of the saints "as if they lived in a world very remote from ours and as though they were free from our struggles, our tensions and fears." Mary's struggles were not unique. She didn't know what the future had in store for her, and she was apprehensive, but she stepped out in faith.

Remove the Cup

We hear strikingly similar words of submission to God's will on the lips of her son, Jesus, years later in the Garden of Gethsemane, on the night before the crucifixion. Jesus sensed what the future held in store for him. He could see himself being brutally stripped, beaten, broken, taunted, and pierced, and dying a horrible, agonizing death. At first he prayed for deliverance from suffering, but his words reveal submission to God's will: "Father, if you are willing, take this cup away from me" (Lk 22:42). And then Jesus' prayer in the garden closes with compelling words of surrender: "Still, not my will but yours be done" (Lk 22:42).

The Sword of Suffering

As Christians, we accept that suffering was part of the Father's plan for Jesus, but we may still struggle to accept God's plan for us, and that is normal. Still, scripture reveals over and over that suffering is inevitable in human life. When Mary went to the Temple carrying her infant in her arms, she met a holy man who told her that her baby was "destined for the fall and rise of many in Israel" (Lk 2:34). He then told her something that any mother would dread hearing—that a sword would pierce her own soul too. She didn't understand the whys and the wherefores, and surely it wasn't easy for her to live with mystery, but she did.

Women with cancer face so many unanswered questions. Why did this happen? What will come next? How long will I live? Will I suffer? Will doctors discover a cure in my lifetime? It is hard to live with mysteries, although our everyday lives overflow with them. Who can explain exactly how caterpillars turn into butterflies or the union of sperm and egg develops into a new human being? Who understands the mystery of tulips lying dormant all winter and emerging triumphantly in springtime? Who knows why one seed will germinate, while another one dies?

Mystery

Mystery was part of life for Mary and Joseph. When they looked for the child Jesus for three days without finding him, Mary was distraught. "Your father and I have been searching for you with great anxiety" (Lk 2:48), she said. And when their beloved child explained his absence by replying, "Did you not know that I must be in my Father's house?" (Lk 2:49), the mother and father were perplexed. "They did not understand what he said to them" (Lk 2:50). As we struggle to accept cancer in our lives, we may sometimes feel like Mary and Joseph. We may not feel that we understand God's message to us.

Joy and Sorrow

No human being escapes drinking from the chalice of suffering. It is true that the cup comes in different disguises. For some, it may be the cup of divorce or widowhood. For others, it may be the chalice of depression or addiction, or the cup of disease or disability. There is no perfect life. However, when you are experiencing especially hard times, it is consoling to realize that the darkest night always births a new dawn. In his book *Can You Drink the Cup?* Henri Nouwen points out that pure sorrow doesn't exist. In the midst of grieving, we suddenly look outside and see a rose in bloom or hear a friend's voice on the phone, and suddenly we taste joy again.

I have a friend in a nursing home who was in a car accident a few years ago and was paralyzed from the neck down. The prospect of her suffering is overwhelming to me, yet my friend has found joy. Although physically immobile, she is spiritually very active. She reads the Bible and prays every day, and although she can't leave the nursing home to minister to others, she does very well in her wheelchair. One day, while I was visiting her, I confessed that I was worried about an upcoming doctor's visit. She looked at me with such kindness and said with conviction, "You'll be fine."

Why Me?

I am sure that my friend went through a long period of asking God, "Why me?" which is a normal response when tragedies strike. When I was undergoing radiation treatments, I had plenty of time to ponder the "Why me?" question. For many years I had been aware that I was in a high-risk category, as the daughter of a woman who had died from breast cancer.

Still, I had expended so much energy over the years eating the "right" foods, taking vitamins, and getting daily exercise that I really felt cheated and let down when I was diagnosed with cancer anyway. I remember talking to a counselor and asking her the question she had probably heard from hundreds of other cancer patients: "Why did this happen to me?" She said, "The body breaks down." But I still grappled with the questions of "Why now?" and "Why me?"

Mystery and the Body

Sometimes we forget that the body is one of life's great, abiding mysteries. Just the fact that I am sitting here at the computer, my brain churning out ideas that are somehow transferred to my fingertips on the keyboard, while my heart pumps blood throughout my body, is a vast miracle. We don't have control over our heartbeat or our kidney functions or our digestive processes. We also don't have control over whether or not we get cancer.

"We don't have complete control over our physical well-being, conscious or unconscious," writes Fr. Robert M. Stewart in *Making Peace With Cancer*. "At times things just go wrong within the incredibly complex human body with all its interrelated organs and systems."

An Ocean of Tears

Tears flowed freely in the weeks following my diagnosis. It seemed that every day I would plant myself on the couch and have a good cry. Eventually, though, I cried every other day, then once a week—and now I may have a good cry only once a month. In looking back, I see that I was grieving over a great sense of loss. I was grieving as I said goodbye to a younger, more carefree, and healthier version of myself, someone who believed that she was in control of her destiny.

Changing Hearts

One story in the gospels helped me see that tears can change hearts. Jesus was having supper at a Pharisee's house when a woman rushed in, quite unexpectedly, and "stood behind him at his feet weeping and began to bathe his feet with her tears" (Lk 7:38). The woman then wiped Jesus' feet with her hair, kissed them, and anointed them. Simon, the host, was upset by her actions, because she had a reputation as a sinful woman, and he thought that Jesus should have known "what sort of woman this is who is touching him, that she is a sinner" (Lk 7:39).

But Jesus defended the woman for her kindness. He told Simon, "When I entered your house, you did not give me water for my feet, but she has bathed them with her tears and wiped them with her hair. You did not give me a kiss, but she has not ceased kissing my feet since the time I entered" (Lk 7:44–45). Jesus then goes on to say the words that reveal his deep compassion: "Her many sins have been forgiven; hence, she has shown great love"(Lk 7: Lk 7:47).

After my diagnosis, I felt such a kinship with that woman. I reflected on how many tears it would take to wash someone's feet, and I wondered where all her tears had come from. I felt like I had cried an ocean of tears myself, and I wondered if the woman might have been ill or perhaps had a child who was ill. It impressed me deeply that the woman used her many tears to bathe Jesus' feet, thereby transforming her sorrow into his comfort. And he gave her a great gift by forgiving her sins and telling her, "Your faith has saved you; go in peace"(Lk 7:50).

The Tears of Jesus

In another story, we see that Jesus himself was not immune to expressions of sorrow. When Jesus arrived at the place where his friend Lazarus lived, everyone was grieving because Lazarus had died. Jesus was described in this scene more than once as "deeply troubled" and "perturbed." And in one of the most beautiful and touching lines in the New Testament, we are told that he was so upset over his friend's death that "Jesus wept" (Jn 11:35).

Tears are a normal part of the cancer journey. Women who have reconstructive surgery after mastectomies may still grieve over a body that has changed irrevocably. Women with uterine or ovarian cancer, who have hysterectomies while still in their childbearing years, may grieve over the loss of their reproductive capabilities. If you are still in the stage of sitting on the couch every day and crying, please keep in mind that grief is a process and does not last forever. The water that flows from your eyes is like a baptism, washing away your fears and worries and helping you become whole again. There will come a day when your grieving is over and you will step out of the shadows and into the light.

Blaming the Victim

We don't get cancer because we thought the wrong thoughts or had the wrong attitude. Breast cancer happens to women who believe in God and to women who don't. It just happens. Unfortunately, sometimes folks will hint that perhaps you are to blame for your illness. People have mentioned my habit of worrying and my former high-stress job. Unfortunately, trying to point the finger of blame at the victim of an illness is not helpful and may increase the psychological torment.

Blaming ourselves can also be part of the cancer journey. When I was first diagnosed, I wracked my brain trying to figure out where I had gone wrong. How in the world had I "let" this happen to me? I was a health food nut. I watched my cholesterol intake and I took antioxidant vitamins, just like the health food gurus recommended. I walked three miles a day and drank filtered water. How could I have come down with cancer? Was it because I'd never had children? Was it because I had stayed too long in a high-stress job? Was it my personality?

The Driver's Seat

At some point, I realized that questions like these rest on an unfounded assumption. They all assume that we are God, all-powerful and all-knowing. They assume that we are in the driver's seat, and that if we eat exactly the right foods and take the right vitamins, we'll attain a state of perfect health. The questions, in effect, are denying God's awesome power in our lives.

In her book, *Seeds of Grace*, Sr. Molly Monahan describes the spiritual and emotional aspects of her journey battling alcoholism. She mentions how important it was for her to surrender to God. She points out that even people who say they believe in God often live as "functional atheists," paying lip service to God but acting as if they were in charge of everything. Surrendering to God can be a crucial move for women with cancer. We must daily acknowledge our dependency on God, who brought us out of the void, who has counted every hair on our head, and who is aware of every breath that we take.

God's Works Made Visible

It is normal to ask, "Why did this happen to me?" when we are hit by an illness, and there is a story in the gospels that explores this question. When Jesus and the disciples encountered a blind man, the disciples asked some questions about suffering that still haunt us today. "Rabbi, who sinned, this man or his parents, that he was born blind?" The disciples were in effect asking Jesus if the man's disability was God's way of punishing the man or his parents. Jesus was adamant in his reply. "Neither he nor his parents sinned." He then went on to explain the underlying spiritual reason for the blindness: "It is so that the works of God might be made visible through him" (Jn 9:1–3).

When I first read that passage, I was perplexed. I couldn't quite grasp the meaning of how the works of God are made visible in a blind man—or in a person with cancer for that matter. However, Jesus went on to heal the man's blindness, so in a very real way he was manifesting God's enormous compassion. Blindness gave Jesus the opportunity to minister to the man, thereby revealing his miraculous healing powers and helping others believe in him.

Healing

God's works are also made visible in breast cancer. Many women, for example, are healed of their illness, and this shows God's awesome power. Other women may not be physically healed, but they may experience spiritual healing and a conversion of heart. Also, God's works are revealed in the compassion of our caregivers, whether they are medical personnel, family members, or friends. The word "compassion" means "to suffer with," and without the dark days of suffering, we would never experience the incredible grace that comes when others relieve our burdens.

If you feel crushed by grief over your suffering, remember that Christ walked among the lame, the sick, the weary, and the dying all his life. Time and again, he ministered to those who were suffering. He revealed the compassionate heart of God each time that he stretched out a hand to help someone up. He is still offering a hand to those who suffer today. That hand is bruised and pierced, but it is a hand that will lift you up, again and again.

Prayer

Jesus, how well I understand your reluctance to drink from the cup of suffering. I too wish I could drink only from the cup of joy, but the cup of sorrow has been handed to me, and even if the taste is bitter, I have hope that I will find glimpses of your loving light in the darkness of cancer. I

trust that you will never abandon me and that
you will always give me a hand to lift me up.
Amen.

Scriptural Reflections and Questions for Discussion

1. Read some of the accounts of healing in the early chapters of Mark: the healing of Simon's mother-in-law in Mark 1:29–31; the healing of the leper in Mark 1:40–42; and the healing of the paralytic in Mark 2:3–5. In each scene, how do the suffering people react to Jesus? How does Jesus react to people who are suffering? How has he responded to your suffering?

2. What people do you know who show enormous grace in suffering?

3. What acts of compassion have you witnessed so far in your cancer journey?

Exercise 1

Jesus invited us to come to him when we are weary and burdened. He said he would give us rest. Draw a simple sketch or write a few paragraphs showing how Jesus is helping you with your burdens.

Exercise 2

Read Luke 7:38–47. Imagine you are the woman in the scene. In your journal, describe your feelings as you wash, anoint, and kiss Jesus' feet. Describe the expression on his face. Imagine what he might say to you.

Five

"If I Hear One More Horror Story, I'll Scream!"

"Take courage, it is I;
do not be afraid."

—Matthew 14:27

It just happened again. Someone stopped by my desk at work and launched into a story about his wife's friend who was diagnosed with breast cancer, was doing fine, and then suffered a recurrence, and the chemotherapy didn't work, and the cancer spread, and the poor

69

woman died. In just a few moments, my mood went from reasonably placid to morose. Since the man knew about my diagnosis, I might have expected him to be more sensitive. Still, I am convinced that he didn't intend to upset me. I believe he was doing what we all do at times, which is talking without having first received a clear "go-ahead" from Brain Central.

Scary Information

Each of us has a different tolerance level for what I call "scary information," and my tolerance is very low. Fortunately, I realized that, even if I didn't have control over the man who stopped by my desk that morning, I did have some control over my reactions. After he went on his merry way, I called my friend Pam and poured out the turmoil in my soul to her. She listened compassionately and said wisely, "That story had nothing to do with you." I could feel the fear in my heart dissolving as she spoke.

Surfing the Web

I have also realized that I have control over the amount of time and energy I devote to filling my head with the latest facts, figures, and theories about cancer. Horror stories seem to be an everyday feature of our society, which sadly suffers from information overload. The Internet is loaded with good, helpful information, but it also overflows with misinformation, unproven theories, and frightening stories. I decided from day one of my illness not to surf the Web for cancer information and not to try to second-guess my doctors.

However, we are all different. If reading information about cancer in books or on the Internet gives you a sense of power, then by all means, go ahead. It is good to keep in mind that certain websites, such as those of the American Cancer Society and the Susan B. Komen Foundation, tend to provide factual and reliable data, while other sites may be loaded with information that is simply someone's best guess. It is important to keep in mind that a delicate balance exists between being informed and being overwhelmed. Only you know where that balance lies in your own heart.

Contradictions

If you do decide to read medical journals or check websites, be prepared for contradictions. For example, for years before my diagnosis I had read articles in health food magazines touting soy products as a protection against breast cancer. Imagine my surprise when I discovered, after my diagnosis, that the medical community disagrees about the effects of soy. Some say the phytoestrogens in soy help protect against breast cancer, while other experts claim these substances may stimulate breast tissue the same way that estrogen does, thus promoting tumor growth.

It's hard to live with ambiguity. We want easy, ready-made answers. But in the case of many cancers, these answers often don't exist. While I was at the radiation therapy center, I discovered a dietary information pamphlet . A study had shown that eating a diet that contains five daily servings of fruit and veggies decreases one's risk of getting cancer. I diligently began chowing down on salads and fruits, until a study came out a few months later that claimed the evidence for the fruit-and-veggies diet was very slim.

For the first few months after my diagnosis, I approached eating with caution and worry. Should I have the chicken or the tuna? The chicken might have traces of antibiotics in it, while the tuna might have mercury. Should I have French fries or not? Were eggs good or bad? The whole issue, of course, boiled down to fear, which can be paralyzing.

Do Not Be Afraid, Mary

The words "fear not" occur more frequently in the New Testament than any other words. When the angel Gabriel visited Zechariah, the poor fellow was terrified and fearful, but the angel reassured him by saying, "Do not be afraid, Zechariah, for your prayer has been heard" (Lk 1:12–13). When the same angel visited Mary, he said, "Do not be afraid, Mary" (Lk 1:30). And later, when the angel appeared to the shepherds, he once again uttered the reassuring words, "Do not be afraid" (Lk 2:10).

Jesus told people "Fear not" over and over and "Don't let your hearts be troubled." Ironically, though, even his friends were unable to quell their fears. Even though they walked and talked with Jesus and broke bread with him, even though they prayed with him day in and day out, they still collapsed into a pit of fear after his death. Luke tells us that when Christ appeared to the apostles after the resurrection, they were in a state of alarm and fright. These men, who lived with Jesus for years, and who saw him raise the dead and heal the sick, still fell prey to the demon of fear.

Irrational Fears

If you're crossing the street and see a truck barreling its way toward you, it's healthy to be fearful and step back. If you see someone suspicious lurking in your backyard at night, your fear will motivate you to seek help. Other fears, however, do nothing to help us. They simply paralyze us. These are the irrational fears, the ones that we create in our own minds, usually in the middle of the night. They are the "what ifs" that we're all so familiar with, as in: *What if my sweetheart leaves me? What if I lose my job? What if the cancer has spread? What if the chemotherapy doesn't work?* And, of course, there is the biggest "what if" of all: *What if I die?*

It might seem logical to assume that we have more fearful situations today than people did during the time Christ lived, since we have the threat of nuclear attack, world war, terrorism, and more diseases than any of us could name. But the gospels reveal plenty of situations that made people anxious: demon possession, leprosy, palsy, hunger, storms, the murder of little children, poverty, blindness, disease, crucifixion, stoning, scourging, and, of course, death. Strangely enough, the disciples were even afraid of Christ. During a raging storm, after they spotted him walking on the sea, they were terrified. They thought Jesus was a ghost, and they cried out in fear.

Prince of Darkness and Fear

When I envision my own fears, I imagine them arising from a place of darkness, and then I remember the one who is known as the Prince of Darkness. It is Satan. As a child, I had a pretty standard version of Satan, as a guy in a red suit with horns and a tail. Today, I believe that Satan is not only the Prince of Darkness but also the Prince of Fear. John tells us, "Perfect love casts out fear," revealing that God, who is perfect love, will always have the final word over Satan.

Still, despite our faith in Jesus, women diagnosed with breast cancer can become entangled in a web of fear. Even though there are many excellent treatments for the illness today and even though the diagnosis is not a death sentence, many women still grapple with the fear of death. "What are the odds that I will survive this illness?" seems a perfectly normal question to me.

The problem is that there are no perfect odds. Perhaps the doctors have told you that the survival rate for women with your particular type of cancer is 85 percent. Well, those are excellent odds, unless you start wondering if you are in the 15 percent who won't make it. There is no way to see the future. To spend time worrying about your future odds is a big waste of the time you have right now. We all realize this on an intellectual level, and yet we are all human, so there will be times when fear gets the best of us.

Women with cancer also grapple with the fear of suffering. I am a terrible coward, and I flinch at the mere thought of syringes, catheters, scalpels, and sutures. And of course I have worried whether the treatments my doctor prescribed for me would be uncomfortable or painful. Like so many other women, I have wondered about the long-term effects of radiation therapy and the medication that I take daily. Most women undergoing treatment for cancer grapple with questions like: *Will I feel ill? Will I feel weak? Will I be able to care for my family? Will I be able to go to work? Will I get my energy back?*

Predicting the Future

The really honest answer to all these questions is "I don't know." It is true that doctors can inform you of the usual side effects of chemotherapy and radiation therapy, but they can't say for sure which side effects you personally will experience. You really won't know what is going to happen until you have undergone the treatments. And no one can really predict the effects of these treatments ten or twenty years down the road.

One doctor warned me that radiation therapy might produce nausea, diarrhea, and fatigue. I was very fortunate, however, since I escaped the dreaded nausea and digestive problems. I have heard of some women who undergo chemotherapy with very little nausea and appetite loss, while other women struggle with these problems. Everyone is different, and no one can predict the future for us.

After my surgery, Jef and I met with Dr. Kennedy in his office to find out what stage and size the tumor had been. As I sat there, braced for an onslaught of bad news, I heard the doctor pronounce the lovely words, "The prognosis is excellent." The tumor had been very small, he explained, and discovered at a very early stage. I was so apprehensive, however, that it took a long time before his words really made an impression on me. Somehow, despite the good news, my fears about cancer were so deeply rooted that anxiety still hounded me. More than three years have passed since the diagnosis, and I still find myself growing anxious before medical appointments. Rationally, I am aware that my illness was detected early and is treatable. But rationality is only one part of a human being. The heart tells a different story. Fear has a way of creeping into our hearts and knocking us off kilter.

The Unknown

So many of our fears are linked to the fact that the future is unknown. If you look at the fear of losing a job very closely, the real answer to "What would happen?" is "I don't know." The future truly is in the hands of God. Is it possible that relatives and friends might come to your aid? Is it possible that another, even better, job might pop up? The answer to all these questions is "I don't know." And the deeper answer is "I trust that God will take care of me."

When I was a child, I believed that trusting God somehow was a guarantee that nothing bad would happen to me. I felt that God and I had a contract of sorts: if I trusted him, he'd protect me from suffering. When both my parents died when I was twenty-nine, I was outraged and heartbroken because I felt God had betrayed his trust. Now, however, I realize that everyone's life comes with crosses. Trusting in God doesn't mean we avoid the crosses. Instead, trusting God is an acknowledgment that he won't abandon us in our times of trial.

Prayer

Heavenly Father, there are times when I feel paralyzed by fears. Help me to see that I needn't give in to the Prince of Darkness, who delights in spreading fear like a virus throughout my soul. Shed your loving light on me so that I will feel your presence even when I am walking in dark shadows of doubt. Shower me with the peace your Son promised to those who believe in him. As I undergo radiation therapy or chemotherapy, please keep me wrapped in your loving arms. Shower me with the grace I need to get through each day, and give me the courage I need to face tomorrow. I pray in Jesus' name. Amen.

Scriptural Reflections and Questions for Discussion

1. Read the scene in Matthew 14:22–33. Why does Peter suddenly feel that he is sinking? What is his cry for help? How does Christ respond? How has Christ responded to you when you have felt yourself sinking in fear?

2. Read Matthew 12:43–45. In what ways do fears sometimes resemble "unclean spirits"? What is Jesus' message to you about the way fears multiply?

3. Read Psalm 32:7, Psalm 18:3, and Psalm
    23:4. What are the Lord's promises to you
    during your illness?

Exercise 1

*Write a letter to Jesus and describe the storms in
your heart. Ask him for help.*

Exercise 2

Make a list of your current fears about cancer.

Exercise 3

*Name your top fears from ten or twenty years ago.
How did the situations turn out? Where was
God's hand?*

Six

Taming Our Fears

"Even the hairs of your head
have all been counted.
Do not be afraid."

—Luke 12:7

*I*n the gospels, Jesus provides plenty of advice about taming fears. "Do not worry about your life, what you will eat (or drink), or about your body, what you will wear," he told his friends. "Is not life more than food and the body more than clothing?" (Mt 6:25).

I have to confess that these words have been hard for me to put into practice in my life. As a little child, I was well aware that my mom was a worrier. Even though the family was blessed by always having food on the table and a roof over our heads, the "poorhouse" loomed large in my mother's worries as she fretted about the future, often expressing fears that we wouldn't have enough. In our family, religion simply meant going to church, and we did not apply the words of Jesus to the everyday workings of our minds or hearts. I don't think any of us ever considered, for example, that true faith and worrying are opposites.

Choking and Strangling

If you look up "worry" in the dictionary, you can see why Jesus warned us against it. Its roots suggest choking and strangling. One of its meanings is "to afflict with mental distress and make anxious," and another meaning is to "touch or disturb something repeatedly." That reminds me of the way we sometimes "worry" a tooth that is troubling us.

When we worry about tomorrow, we are disturbing our peace of mind and casting a cloud of gloom on today. We jump onto a negative train of thought and refuse to get off. When you have a chronic illness like cancer, your train of thought can take you to frightening destinations, and it becomes a real test of faith to stay in the present moment as much as possible.

Lessons From the Birds

Jesus reminded us that the birds and the beasts teach us some vital lessons about living. "Look at the birds in the sky; they do not sow or reap, they gather nothing into barns, yet your heavenly Father feeds them. Are not you more important than they?"(Mt 6:26). It is true, of course, that when we look at the natural world, we see how wonderfully God provides, and how fully dependent birds and squirrels and rabbits are on an unseen providence. A bird or a squirrel knows how to seek food and how to make a nest through instinct, which is one of those mysteries in nature that point to the existence of a loving God.

Human beings are not so fortunate. Most of us have lost the ability to provide our own food, and we rely on others to build our "nests" or houses. We get what we need through the sweat of our brow, and it is sometimes tempting to think that we are the ones in control. But Jesus tells us that our Heavenly Father feeds the birds, and then he asks, "Are not you more important than they?" to remind us that it is God who provides for us too. If we have a job and use the money to buy food and pay rent, we may think we are the providers, but the job is evidence of God's providence.

Life Span

Jesus asks, "Can any of you by worrying add a single moment to your life-span?" (Mt 6:27). This question has echoed in my heart countless times since my diagnosis. Cancer makes you wonder how much more time you have. There is no answer to the question, since our life spans are in God's hands, but modern medicine can tempt us into believing that if we get the right doctor and the latest treatments, we can control the number of days we have left on Planet Earth.

Seeking a good doctor and excellent treatment makes perfect sense, of course, but some people face a moment when they have to decide whether the treatments are worth the agony. My friend Marty reached this point when she suffered a recurrence of cancer that had spread to her brain. The treatments might have given her a few extra months of life, although that was very uncertain, and the doctors admitted that she would suffer severe side effects. In a tremendous act of faith and surrender, Marty decided to stop the treatments. She spent the last few months of her life enjoying her family and sitting outside on the deck, listening to the birds, praying, and spending time with friends. Her daughter reported that my friend died peacefully, and without pain.

Tomorrow

"Do not worry about tomorrow," Jesus said. "Tomorrow will take care of itself" (Mt 6:34). These words speak so lovingly to women with cancer. Worrying about tomorrow robs us of the precious moments we have today. I have spent so much time in my life worrying about events that never took place, and I have also worried that I would not be able to handle tragedies when they occurred, such as my parents' deaths. Time and again, though, God has shown me the futility of worrying. When my parents died—only six months apart—God provided everything I needed to get through the experience.

Tying Up Loose Ends

You may worry about your children, your husband, and perhaps other beloved people in your life. "What would happen if I die?" I have wondered numerous times since the diagnosis. "Will my husband be all right?" I don't have children, but I can imagine how my thoughts would run if I did. Cancer is not a death sentence, but it is a very strong reminder of our mortality. It calls us to tie up loose ends in our lives and to stop procrastinating about the things that really matter. If you have dependent children, then of course it makes sense to talk with your husband about what would happen if you should die, but there is no need to dwell too long on death.

Seeking the Kingdom

We have to keep going back to the words of Jesus. He admonishes us to "Seek first the kingdom [of God] and his righteousness, and all these things will be given you besides" (Mt 6:33). The things he is talking about are food and drink and clothing, the necessities of life. Our lives are in the hands of God, and we can't change God's plan for us by worrying. Worrying actually robs us of the life we have now because it diminishes the pleasure of the present moment, which is the only moment we have for sure. The past is gone, and the future is but a dream.

Jesus showed us other ways to tame our fears and conquer our worries. "I have come that they might have life and have it abundantly," he said, and he himself lived abundantly by fishing, sharing meals with friends, attending weddings, healing the sick, ministering to the heartbroken, and praying. Living abundantly and living fearfully are contradictory, because fears constrict us and dull the edge of the beautiful here and now.

Little Children

There are many keys to living joyfully and fearlessly in the gospels, but one that really hits home with me is Jesus' admonition that we must experience a major change of heart. "Whoever does not accept the kingdom of God like a child will not enter it," Jesus said (Mk 10:15). These are tough words, especially for folks with jobs and family responsibilities. We have to pay the utility and water bills, cover the mortgage, fill out the medical insurance forms, make the next doctor's appointment, and fill the cupboard with food. How can we be childlike?

It's important to note that there is a world of difference between being childlike and being childish. Childish people are selfish and demanding and rarely live up to their obligations, while childlike people are open, trusting, loving, and spontaneous. Childlike people get the bills paid, but they also take time to clip a rose from the garden and enjoy a freshly baked cookie. They are not so bogged down by the demands of adult life that they forget to notice the clouds in the sky or the song of a bird at dawn.

My friends have a four-year-old girl whom I think of as my little spiritual director. This girl thoroughly enjoys every moment, whether she is picking flowers, eating cake, or playing games. She doesn't remember too much about yesterday, and she rarely frets over tomorrow. She lives in the here and now.

Children enjoy the simple things in life. As any mom can attest, it really doesn't take much to amuse a small child. A pie tin and a spoon can provide hours of fun, and a newborn flower or a fancy butterfly is a great thrill. Jesus was calling us to remember the simple joys when he advised us to become childlike. The simple joys are free and they are all around us. Even if we are undergoing radiation therapy or chemotherapy, we can enjoy a flower, nuzzles from a puppy, a sunset, or a hug.

Trust

Children are also trusting. My friend's little girl sits in the back seat of the car and lets her mom do the driving. She doesn't worry about car wrecks or running out of gas or getting lost. At night if she has a nightmare, she trusts that her mom or dad will come to her rescue. Many adults might protest that they can't be childlike because they no longer have adults to come to their rescue. But Jesus was letting us know that if we place our trust in God, we will always be rescued.

Saying Thank-You

Gratitude is another way to tame our fears and calm our hearts. Little children may not know the words "thank-you," but they reveal gratitude in the pleasure they take in life's little joys, like a new flower or a snazzy seashell. It is wonderful to be grateful when God grants our big wishes, like a promotion at work, or a fun-filled vacation, but it helps to see that he is sending us little gifts every moment of the day.

On a wonderful website, www.gratefulness.org, Br. David Steindl-Rast, O.S.B., reminds us that gratefulness can heal a negative spirit. "In each of us there is a spark that can reverse the trends of violence and depression spiraling within us and in the world around us," he writes. He suggests that gratitude helps us journey toward peace and joy.

Our lives are brimming with reasons to be grateful, even when we are burdened with illness. We sample many joys every day, whether they are a delicious brownie, a friend's smile, or a baby's giggle. When I'm feeling gloomy, I remind myself of how grateful I am that someone invented coffee and chocolate. I am also grateful that God gave birds the ability to sing and lightning bugs the magical talent of illuminating dark summer nights.

Many of us might protest that our personalities don't allow us to be childlike. We have forgotten what it means to be spontaneous and grateful and joyful. We may feel so burdened by our illness that we can't seem to tap into that childlike nature that we once had. I have a very hard time being childlike because I tend to be a worrier with a high-control personality, so I am praying to Jesus for the gift of a childlike heart. After all, he was the one who said, "With God anything is possible."

The Busy Train of Thoughts

One way to follow Jesus' advice to "stop worrying about tomorrow" is by learning how to rein in our busy train of thoughts. If you are relaxing on your back deck and enjoying a nice supper with your spouse or sweetheart, you may suddenly feel your mind zooming into the future. "Oh, no, I have another biopsy tomorrow." Or "Oh, no, I have to go for radiation tomorrow." Or "Next week is my mammogram." Your mind has pulled you away from the lovely present moment into a nebulous future, which is unknown.

I've had success controlling my fretful train of thoughts by repeating mentally, "This moment, the one right now, is fine." Take a few deep breaths as you repeat this phrase. The present moment may be filled with the lovely sounds of birdsong or music. Perhaps you are munching on a delicious piece of bread and sipping lemonade. Don't allow worries to spoil your joy.

Drawing Closer to Jesus

Jesus said to first seek the kingdom of God, and we do that by loving and enjoying life, loving God and our neighbor, and enjoying the wonders of God's creation. We also seek the kingdom by drawing closer to Jesus, which we can do by reading the gospels, since the stories reveal Jesus' love and mercy and give us hope. I try to read scriptures in an active way. You do this by using your imagination as you read and putting yourself into the scenes.

For example, when Jesus invites the children to come to him, you might imagine yourself as one of the children running up to him. Imagine what you would talk to him about and how he might reply. In another gospel story, you might envision yourself as the woman who anoints his feet with precious oil. Open your heart to Jesus and tell him about your concerns, especially about your illness. He will listen.

Jesus told us that the kingdom of God is within our hearts, and that is where he resides too. He is the

Prince of Peace, and he came to bring us joy and love. When we are struggling with fears, he understands us. He always keeps the promise "Peace be with you." He always tames our fears.

Prayer

Lord, you know every inch of my heart. You know how easy it is for me to fall into the pit of fear and worry. Help me to keep my mind on the present moment. Help me to recognize that the future is unknown, and the past is over. All I have is the present moment, which is so precious. Help me to become like a little child, putting my life entirely in your hands, and enjoying all the wonderful gifts you send me each day, whether it is a fancy sunrise, a new flower, a child's hug, a delicious meal, or a lovely song. Especially during the days of my treatments for cancer, let me practice gratitude for all the little things that still give me joy. Help me to trust that you will take care of the big things. Amen.

Scriptural Reflections and Questions for Discussion

1. What does becoming childlike mean to you? What changes might you make in your life to become more childlike?

2. Read 1 John 4:18 and 1 John 4:7–9. What is the relationship between fear and love? How has love overcome fear in your life?

3. In Psalm 27:5–10, what does God promise you?

4. Isaiah 43:1–4, 18–19 is a lovely passage to read aloud when you are frightened or distressed.

5. Read Matthew 8:23–27 and then describe the storms in your heart. Ask Jesus to calm them.

Exercise 1

Practice gratefulness each day. Make a list of some ordinary joys and pleasures in your life that you are grateful for. These don't have to be dramatic or fancy or expensive!

Exercise 2

Take a favorite story from the New Testament and explore it in an active way by putting yourself into the scene. Perhaps you are Peter taking the Lord's hand and walking on water. Or perhaps you are with Jesus at the wedding feast in Cana, when he turns water into wine. Imagine talking with Jesus and listening to him.

Part Three

Embracing the Light of Christ: Recovery

"I am the light of the world."

—John 8:12

*R*ecovering from the shock of a cancer diagnosis does not happen overnight. There may be moments when you feel you'll never be free of worry and stress. I confess that I've gone through many boxes of Kleenex since my diagnosis, but as someone who has logged over three years since that fateful day, I assure you that it does get better.

For the first few months, though, you may find yourself dwelling on the diagnosis and reliving the events of surgery and other treatments. This is perfectly normal. But I promise you that there will come a day when your diagnosis is not the first thing on your mind when you wake up in the morning. There will come a day when you step out of the shadows and bask again in the light of Christ's joy.

The simple question "How are you?" can be tricky for a woman recovering from cancer. Some people who ask are only being polite, but others really do want to know. Since my diagnosis, I've tried to keep my answers brief since I doubted that anyone, except a few close friends, wanted a lengthy dissertation on my physical and mental state. Still, I didn't want to lie to people who really cared. So, when they asked how I was, I explained that physically I was feeling fine, but emotionally and spiritually the struggles were not over.

Recovery from cancer is not merely a physical process; it also has emotional and spiritual undertones. I feel like I am in very good physical shape, but emotionally, I am still healing. Although I dwell on my illness much less than I did during the first few months following diagnosis, cancer is never completely gone from my consciousness. Someone described cancer as a whale that comes to sit in your living room and seems to dominate your whole life. As the months go on, you tend to notice the whale less and less, but you are always aware that the whale is still there.

I have a daily reminder of the whale in the small white pill that I take every morning, a pill that is touted as helping prevent cancer's recurrence. I will not be totally "out of the woods" until I reach the five-year mark, in May 2005, when I will no longer take this medication. Other reminders of my particular whale are surgeons' visits (at first every three months, now every six), plus a yearly mammogram and visits to the radiologist.

Even though chances of recurrence in my situation are extremely low, no one can assure me that I am 100 percent healed. I remind myself, however, that no one has a 100 percent guarantee of waking up tomorrow, nor do any of us have a guarantee that we will make it through the day. One blessed insight that cancer brings is the recognition that none of us knows how many years we have left on the planet, and it's best to accomplish tasks that we feel God is calling us to do while we are healthy enough to tackle them.

There have been distinct stages in my spiritual journey with cancer. During the diagnosis and treatment stages, I was almost completely engulfed in worries about myself. I look back and envision myself as someone sailing in a boat that was barely seaworthy. I was so busy bailing out water and trying to keep myself afloat that if another boat near me had been capsizing, I doubt I would have been much help. At some point my perspective changed, although I am not sure of the exact day. I just know that I began to have more good days than bad, and I began once again enjoying looking around at the sea of life and noticing the many funny and touching things that were happening. Today, I feel I am finally at the point where I might give a hand to other boaters who are in danger of sinking.

In *Making Peace With Cancer*, Fr. Stewart rejects the title of "cancer survivor," because he feels that the word "survivor" overlooks the moments of grace that he has experienced in facing his illness. I have to agree with him. To me, the word "survivor" sounds like someone who barely escaped from a plane wreck or a burning house. In the old days, people who had cancer were called "cancer victims," but the word "victim" is too harsh, and today we have a whole slew of "survivors" in our world. Maybe the truth lies somewhere in between. All of us, whether we have cancer or not, are survivors in the most basic senses. We have survived the ailments of childhood that kill so many in underdeveloped nations. Some of us have survived serious car accidents, and others have survived unhappy marriages.

I don't know what noun I would suggest in place of "survivor" in referring to people who have navigated the rough waters of a cancer diagnosis, and are now in recovery. Rather than being known as a survivor, I think I'd rather be known as a woman in recovery, or a woman with cancer that is in remission. Those are longer titles than "survivor," but I like their sound better.

The next few chapters give pointers about recovering spiritually from cancer. Even if your diagnosis was many years ago, I think you will still find meaning in this part of the book. Carving out time every day for prayer, spending time in silence, and learning some special ways of loving and serving others will help you journey from darkness to light, from sorrow to joy, and from chaos to peace.

Seven

Healing Our Hearts

In the morning,
while it was still very dark, he got up
and went out to a deserted place, and
there he prayed.

—Mark 1:35 (NRSV)

*C*ancer can unleash chaos in our lives. Plans, big and little, have to be revamped or ditched to make room for surgery, chemotherapy, and/or radiation therapy. Suddenly we find ourselves tearing up many to-do lists, as we devote our energy to getting well.

Prayer is a crucial way to heal our hearts during recovery from cancer, a time period that varies depending on the individual. Some people still call themselves "survivors" even twenty years after the diagnosis, while others might prefer to drop the title much earlier than that. Recovery can refer to the physical healing that occurs as you are getting over radiation or chemotherapy, but it also refers to spiritual and emotional healing, which sometimes take longer.

Golden Moments of Silence

Praying in silence has been especially healing during my recovery phase, since it has given me a chance to turn off my busy mind and rest in God's presence. For some folks, though, silence can be a frightening prospect. We live in such a busy world, where cell phones jingle all around us, car horns honk, televisions and radios blare. For moms, there is the bawling of an infant, the endless questions of a toddler, or the chatter of a child. Above us, planes roar through the sky. To our left and right, neighbors blaze paths through their lawns with growling machines that shatter the stillness. At the grocery store, canned music hounds us.

Island Retreat

Often we fear solitude and silence because we suspect that they may unleash frightening or upsetting memories or ideas, and we try to keep those images at bay by bathing ourselves in a constant stream of noise. But silence is enormously healing and essential to achieving balance in the soul. *Gift From the Sea* is a beautiful book that Anne Morrow Lindbergh wrote while she was taking an island retreat, apart from her husband and children. She underscores the importance of silence and solitude for women:

> Certain springs are tapped only when we are alone. The artist knows he must be alone to create; the writer to work out his thoughts; the musician to compose. . . . But women need solitude in order to find again the true essence of themselves. . . .

In Mary's life, silence was so important. When the angel Gabriel came to her with his amazing announcement, she had to receive his words with an open and silent heart. Each of us has little "annunciations" in our lives every day, but unless we spend time in solitude, we may miss hearing God's messages to us. As Mother Teresa noted in *No Greater Love,* "In the silence of the heart, God speaks."

In today's world, long periods of silence can make us antsy. Constant chatter assures us that we have company. People who live alone often keep the radio or TV on all the time, as a way to prevent themselves from facing their solitude. Trying to evade silence works for a while, but there always comes the unavoidable moment of confrontation. You may awaken at three o'clock in the morning to head to the bathroom, and then find yourself fully awake and alone with your thoughts once you get back in bed.

Being Still

"Be still and know that I am God," says the psalmist, reminding us that God is found within the stillness in our hearts. Elijah looked for God in the wind, an earthquake, and in fire, but he found God in "a tiny whispering sound." (1 Kgs 19:9, 11–13). Jesus told us the kingdom of heaven is within our hearts, but unless we give ourselves the gift of silence, it is difficult to tap into that kingdom. He also told us that his sheep always recognize his voice, but we won't be able to hear the voice of God unless we take a break from all the noise in our lives.

Retreating

In the gospels, Jesus is usually pictured among crowds of people, but he also took time to retreat to the mountain, the desert, or the sea, where he could pray in solitude. He showed us by example that there is a time to pray with others and a time to pray alone. There is a time to make a joyful noise unto the Lord, when we are gathered with our community at church, and there is a time for quiet, meditative prayer.

Spending time alone with Jesus in the desert is a wonderful way to recover your emotional and spiritual equilibrium after a cancer diagnosis. You can mimic the desert experience by taking a weekend retreat at a monastery or retreat house, where you can leave behind all cares and responsibilities, but you can also have a retreat in your own home.

Prayer in the Center

I have tried creating my own little desert of peace and silence in my life by setting aside time each day to pray the way Jesus recommended when he said, "When you pray, go to your inner room, close the door, and pray to your Father in secret" (Mt 6:6). In a book called *Intimacy With God*, I learned about an ancient type of Christian prayer called centering prayer. The author, Thomas Keating, recommends choosing a sacred word like "love," "Christ," "Jesus," or "peace." Then you find a quiet and comfortable place to sit, and you close your eyes. Each time a swarm of thoughts, worries, or fears threatens to overtake you, you calmly repeat your sacred word. The sacred word expresses our intention to love God, writes Fr. Keating, to be in God's presence, and "to submit to the Spirit's action during the time of prayer."

Generally, it is good to practice centering prayer for fifteen to twenty minutes in the morning and fifteen to twenty minutes in the afternoon. If you have small children at home, it may be a challenge to find blocks of time to devote to centering prayer, but you may be able to find prayer time after the children are tucked away in bed—or perhaps during their nap times.

Spaces Between Thoughts

Centering prayer is wonderful for spiritual healing. It helps you find that peace-filled "inner room" that Jesus mentioned. Even though we often identify ourselves with the flurries of thoughts and worries that fill our minds day in and day out, the practice of centering prayer reveals the spaces between thoughts, the moments when we have no thoughts at all. These moments reveal that we are something more than just a collection of ideas, memories, doubts, fears, and future projections—and in this realization is a release from mental suffering, fears, and worries.

"We have thoughts, but we are not our thoughts," Fr. Keating explains. "Most people suffer because they think they are their thoughts and if their thoughts are distressing, upsetting or evil, they are stuck with them." When we stop thinking, even for a few moments a day, we gradually see that we don't have to be dominated by our thoughts. And this can be a great revelation for a woman who feels that her thoughts about cancer, her concerns about the future, or her worries about her health are taking over her life.

Adoring God

In *The Way of the Heart*, Henri J. M. Nouwen writes about meeting Mother Teresa and asking her advice about how he could become a good priest. Her answer was simple enough: "Spend one hour a day in adoration of your Lord and never do anything you know is wrong. . . ." Nouwen understood her words to mean that a direct and intimate encounter with Jesus was an essential starting point of his ministry. He describes solitude as the place where our salvation will occur, a place "where Christ remodels us in his own image and frees us from the victimizing compulsions of the world."

Turning Off the Tube

Getting rid of the TV set can also be a big step in your spiritual and emotional recovery from cancer. Unfortunately, the TV can be a source of major anxiety in our lives, and it is certainly not a healing presence. Even people who claim that they "only watch the news" are inviting horrible scenes of carnage and misery into their living rooms. Yes, we need to be informed about what is happening in the world, but when we are faced with bloody scenes on a daily basis, we are in danger of increasing the level of anxiety in our lives, while also becoming immune to suffering. Another big problem with TV is that it drains away time that could be used for praying, scriptural reading, playing with children, and ministering to family and friends who are in need. Many people who say they have no time to garden, do volunteer work, pray, bake bread, or take walks somehow find four hours a day to sit in front of the tube.

Going Outdoors

Nature is a great source of healing. Jesus spent most of his time outdoors and often slipped away to the mountain, the desert, or the sea to pray. As you are recovering from cancer, it is essential to find special places in the natural world where prayer and silence come naturally for you. For many years, my husband and I enjoyed vacationing on a small island in the Gulf of Mexico, where we would enjoy tooling around in a small, simple boat equipped with a quiet electric engine.

We would head into the marshes each morning to sit there in absolute silence, noticing every sound that Mother Nature makes when she is not drowned out by the cacophony of human beings. We could hear pistol shrimp making delicate popping noises under the boat and hear the rowdy splashes of nearby otters. These little excursions into the marshes were healing and prayerful, and helped us feel closer to God.

Sacred Spaces

You don't have to go boating, however, to find sacred places. You will discover them in your own neighborhood and your own backyard, if you just look. As you are recovering from chemotherapy or radiation therapy, take the time to discover sacred spaces in the midst of your everyday life. Taking a walk in silence through a forest or park or quietly sitting by a creek can help you feel God's healing presence. If you have a porch where you can sit and listen to the birds and the squirrels, make that your little chapel of solitude and healing.

I think it is worth noting that when God created our first parents, he placed them in a garden, not in a hut, cave, or house (or mall!) The scenes in Genesis overflow with natural imagery, like floods, wild animals, birds, wind, rain, fruit, and trees. The New Testament shines with stories of Jesus enjoying nature. You see him fishing, wandering in the desert, and climbing the mountain. His parables brim with natural images like lambs, lilies, mustard seeds, fig trees, vines, sparrows, and fish. He was a carpenter, who used his hands to fashion things from wood.

Despite our cell phones, beepers, and faxes, despite air conditioning and wall-to-wall carpeting, we still are a part of nature today. Our bodies respond to the cycles of the moon, the rising and falling of the barometer, changes in light and darkness, and the seasons. As Marjorie Kinnan Rawlings so beautifully expressed it in *Cross Creek*: "We were bred of the earth. And something shrivels in a man's soul when he turns his back on nature and concerns himself only with the things of men."

Roses and Birdfeeders

You don't have to take up wilderness camping to discover the deep healing power of nature. Even the simplest activities that get you in touch with nature can connect you with the Creator. Clipping roses in the garden, picking blueberries, pulling a few weeds, and collecting shells are all remarkable antidotes to the blues and can help you heal your heart.

Even if you live in a high-rise in the middle of a big city, you can head to a park where you can feed the ducks and squirrels. Or you might fling open your window and study the sky. Notice how cloud formations change every second, and how often the moving clouds resemble the sea. If you are fortunate enough to live near the sea, head to the shore and observe the sea's lovely responses to the swelling and dwindling of the moon.

Lifting Up Your Heart

Church is a lovely place to lift up our hearts to God, but in my recovery from cancer, I've discovered other places that are also heart nurturing and healing. My husband and I go to the Atlanta zoo about once a month. Even though we don't have kids, we still enjoy watching the elephant and bird shows, petting the potbellied pigs, and giggling at the antics of the gorillas. About once a year we visit a nature center in Homosassa Springs, Florida, where we watch the manatees happily devouring cabbages and carrots.

Seeds of Hope

It can be spiritually healing to grow something, whether it's tomatoes, peppers and lettuce, or just a few simple herbs. If you don't have much land, you might try planting a few flower seeds or bulbs in pots on a sunny window or porch. Planting a seed, watering it, and then watching it burgeon into a vegetable or flower can provide a beacon of hope and rebirth. Adding a birdfeeder to your life can bring hours of amusement, and the animals will be grateful for your efforts. One of my favorite activities is watching the squirrel that has taken up residence in a birdhouse in our yard. On rainy days, I often see his sleepy little face poking out, and some days all I see is his tail blowing in the breeze.

When you feel yourself sinking into the cycle of "poor me," as in "Poor me, I have cancer" or entangled in the dreaded web of "what ifs," as in, "What if it recurs?" you might want to try following in the footsteps of our beloved Jesus and heading outdoors. Start with the basics, like taking a short walk. When I'm strolling around the block, stopping to pet neighborhood cats, greet neighbors, and admire babies and puppies, I lose the whole train of thought that is centered on "what if" and "poor me." When you get a dose of Mother Nature, you realize you are a part of a much bigger plan and there is a Big Planner at the helm.

Prayer

Jesus, during the years that you lived among us, you were so generous to the sick and ailing. You were moved by compassion to heal the lepers, the lame, and the blind. One woman was too shy to actually ask for healing; instead, she touched the hem of your robe. And that was enough, because you felt her touch and knew of her deep faith. In my recovery from cancer, I am also touching the hem of your robe, dear One. I am sitting silently and basking in the warmth of your love. Please heal me physically, spiritually, and emotionally. Please take me in your arms and help me to feel whole once again. Amen.

Scriptural Reflections and Questions for Discussion

1. Read Psalm 39:1–3 and Proverbs 10:19. What messages are there about silence? How can you get more silence in your everyday life?

2. Describe your sacred spaces, where you especially feel God's presence.

3. Read the two creation stories in chapters 1 and 2 of Genesis. Note how many images of nature there are. How do you connect with nature in your everyday life?

Exercise 1

Declare a TV-free day, and then a TV-free week. Record the activities you did instead of watching the tube, and observe your emotional state.

Exercise 2

Plant a few seeds or bulbs. Try tulips, wildflowers, broccoli, basil or other herbs. If you don't have a yard, plant the seeds in a pot and put the pot in a sunny window.

Exercise 3

Carve out time each day to be alone and pray in silence.

Eight

Finding Grace
in the Cross

"This is how all will know that you
are my disciples, if you have
love for one another."

—John 13:35

*I*n her book *No Greater Love,* Mother Teresa
relates a beautiful little story about a robin.
When the robin saw Jesus suffering on the
cross, the bird flew around and around until he
could remove a thorn from the crown piercing
Jesus' head. As he did, the thorn pierced the little

bird, and the robin's breast turned red from the blood. "Each of us should be that little bird. We should ask ourselves what we have done to comfort others," Mother Teresa writes. "When I look at the cross, I think of that robin," she adds. "Don't pass by the cross. It is a place of grace."

Denying the Cross

Seeing grace in our own crosses can be a real challenge. At first, I was very reluctant to pick up my cross, and the notion of finding even the faintest glimmer of light or love there was foreign to me. Frankly, I was in denial about my illness. I kept expecting the doctor to call me to say there had been a big mistake, and I was really in perfectly good health. I knew that Jesus had said, "If anyone would come after me, he must deny himself, take up his cross, and follow me" (Mt 16:24), but I wasn't ready. "Please, Jesus, can't you give me a lighter cross?" I begged.

As time passed, however, I began observing other people who seemed to be discovering light in the darkness of their suffering, and they helped me emerge from my state of denial. I have a middle-aged friend who is gradually losing her vision due to a degenerative eye disease. When she first learned about her condition, she seemed terribly shaken and overwhelmed by grief and fear over the prospect of going blind, but then, as the weeks progressed, I noticed that she seemed calm and joyful. Her good humor had returned, and she was optimistic again. Wondering if she had found grace in her cross, I asked her about her secret. "My husband and I have been reading the scriptures together every day," she said. "It makes such a difference."

Embracing Jesus

Gradually, I started seeing glimmers of light in my own situation. It helped to reflect on the kind and compassionate people who were helping me through the diagnosis. Before my world had been turned upside down by cancer, I had often longed to have a spiritual director, someone with whom I could discuss my spiritual journey, but I kept procrastinating. After I discovered that I had cancer, I sent a letter to a well-known and respected priest and spiritual director in Atlanta and asked if he would counsel me.

I had heard that he was a very busy man, and deep in my heart I was preparing myself for rejection. How surprised and moved I was when he wrote back and told me that he would be honored to see me. We meet about once a month and discuss all the twists, turns, and potholes of my spiritual life. He has given me, time and again, the gift of listening by allowing me to feel free to pour out my deep-seated fears and worries, with no holds barred. One day I was feeling particularly troubled and asked his guidance, and he looked at me with infinite kindness and said, "You have to throw yourself into the arms of Jesus over and over." That comforting image returned to me many times in the months that followed.

My life has been filled with so much grace since my illness. One afternoon, I heard the screen door opening and heard Pam and her little boy, Stephen, then six, coming in. He was carrying a plate of cookies that he and his grandma had made, plus a hand-drawn card. For the rest of my life, I will remember the shy and loving look on the little boy's face as he handed me his offerings. Another day, I was returning from the radiotherapy clinic and feeling rather gloomy as I contemplated the five weeks of treatments still ahead of me. My spirits soared when I discovered a gift bag on the front porch in which my friend Kevin had nestled a very plush stuffed cat, which still brightens my days.

Light of Christ

Reading the scriptures, especially the accounts of Jesus' death, has also helped me. As Christians, we see images of the crucifixion so often that sometimes I feel we are in danger of forgetting how agonizing Christ's death must have been. He was impaled with a crown of thorns, scourged, stripped, mocked, and spat upon, and then suffered the agony of having nails driven through his flesh. Still, in the midst of incomparable suffering and at a time that seemed like the darkest moment of his life, Jesus showed compassion. Nothing could dim the love of Christ.

One of the thieves dying next to Jesus made a very humble request. "Jesus, remember me when you come into your kingdom" (Lk 23:42). It was such a simple request. The man didn't ask for a special place in the kingdom, just to be remembered. And Jesus responded immediately in the most compassionate way possible and comforted the man with the words "Today you will be with me in paradise." Jesus also brought a glimmer of light to his beloved mother, who was experiencing what had to be a mother's worst nightmare, standing beneath the cross, watching her beloved child die. The disciple John was also there, and Jesus, wanting to ensure that Mary would be cared for after his death, said to Mary, "Woman, behold, your son." And then he said to John, "Behold, your mother" (Jn 19:26–27). From that day forward, John took Mary into his home and took care of her.

Connecting With Others

As we struggle to accept the cross of cancer, we may be too weary at first to do much good for other people. At some point, however, when we regain our energy and start looking around, we may discover that so many of our friends and family members are struggling with heartache or suffering. The cross we carry may seem like the heaviest one in the world, but plenty of people are bent under the weight of heavier ones. It has taken me time to see this, but I believe that cancer can be a place of grace once we feel a connection with all the other people in the world who are suffering.

Serving Others

I was so touched by the many outpourings of kindness from friends and family that I was eager to show my love for others. So, when radiation therapy was well behind me, I began casting about for ways to serve. I had been a minister to shut-ins and the elderly at my church for a few years, and I knew I wanted to continue that ministry, but I felt that God might be calling me to other types of service. It was difficult to choose, however, among the cafeteria line of opportunities that exist in the metro Atlanta area. Did I want to volunteer in the kindergarten of my church's school? Did I want to be a tutor? Did I want to work in a hospital? Did I want to serve at a homeless shelter or pitch in at the American Cancer Society?

Sharing Our Gifts

I tried on a few different hats. I volunteered at the school for a short time and tried my hand delivering flowers at the hospital, but these activities left me feeling drained. Then one day, Fr. Pavol Brenkus, a priest at my church, delivered a homily exploring the question of how we can best serve God and our neighbors. He mentioned the importance of using the unique gifts that God has given us in our service to others.

What Is Mine to Do?

Over the next few weeks, I spent time in prayer, trying to discover my gifts. As I prayed, I had some insights. Flower delivery had been fun, I realized, but perhaps because it didn't come naturally to me, I had tired of it quickly. Volunteering at the school had been enjoyable, but that didn't seem to be my calling either. One day, I was reading about St. Francis of Assisi and discovered that, on his deathbed, he had said to his friends, "I have found what is mine to do. May Christ help you find what is yours to do." At that moment, I felt very strongly that Christ would help me find what unique service he was calling me to. I just had to be patient.

When I reflected on the gifts that I enjoyed using, writing was definitely at the top of the list. Gradually, I realized that I could use that gift to serve others by writing a book about my cancer journey. A short time later, I thought about another talent, one that had revealed itself in my younger days when I had taught college English and philosophy—the gift of teaching. Again, reflecting on cancer as a new bend in the road of my life, I realized that I could minister to others by launching a prayer group at my church for women with cancer.

You may be reading these lines and thinking, "I am too exhausted or weak to even consider helping someone else"—and that's fine. It is really important to be patient with yourself as you recover from cancer. Energy and enthusiasm may escape you for a while, but they will return. At some point in your journey, you will wake up feeling energetic and renewed, and you will know that you are ready for the next stage of healing, which is service.

Mothering as Ministry

I have to add a word of caution. Often we feel that our calling is something more than we are doing at the time, and we may overlook our most obvious gifts and talents. For example, if you are a full-time mother, and your day is filled with cooking, cleaning, watching the children, overseeing activities, organizing play groups, and generally striving to keep your children healthy and happy, then your way of feeding the Lord's little sheep is through mothering, which is a lovely calling.

You may, of course, have other gifts, and these can lead to other ministries. My friend Pam always knew that she wanted to be a mom, and she and her husband have made sacrifices so she can stay at home with their two children. But God also blessed Pam with an exquisite soprano voice, a gift that she shares with others by singing in the church choir, and leading the children's choir at Christmas.

If you are trying to discern what your gifts are, don't overlook your hobbies, interests, and passions. My friend Margaret is a nurse practitioner who loves baking in her spare time, and she ministers to friends who are ill, as well as to friends celebrating happy occasions, by showing up at the door with an armful of scrumptious brownies, bread, or cookies.

Some women who are recovering from cancer still have very full schedules. Some are tending to elderly relatives at home, while also raising children. Some are working full-time outside the home. You can minister at home by making a cup of tea or lending an ear to someone in trouble, and you can minister at work by little acts of kindness too. I work part-time in a library, where my colleagues frequently bring in home-baked muffins, brownies, or produce from their gardens to share with others. These little gifts brighten the workday and lift people's spirits.

Watch Your Heart

We are blessed with so many gifts. Some of us have talents like the ability to sew and knit, while others can paint, play music, sing, write, or cook. Some of us are natural born gardeners, and others are wonderful at taking care of children or the elderly. Our hearts act as barometers to let us know if we are trying to shoehorn our personality into a ministry that really doesn't suit us.

Years ago, I did a short stint as a volunteer at an AIDS home for women, which was run by Mother Teresa's nuns, and I noticed that the sisters were always smiling and cheerful, even though they were dealing with serious illness and death on a daily basis. I didn't experience joy, however, when I volunteered there. Instead, I felt very anxious about making a mistake and very sad about the suffering. Using my heart as a barometer, I realized that I wasn't suited to that ministry.

Small Acts of Love

We don't have to do huge service projects to show our love for others. Sometimes just the smallest acts of kindness make a huge difference. St. Thérèse of Lisieux, also known as the Little Flower, wrote about the little way of love in her autobiography, *The Story of a Soul*. Thérèse had numerous health problems, and at first she fretted that these would prevent her from serving God. "Love proves itself by deeds, and how shall I prove mine?" she wrote in her diary. "Great deeds are forbidden me."

Gradually, though, Thérèse realized that she could show her love in small ways. "I can prove my love only by scattering flowers, that is to say, by never letting slip a single little sacrifice, a single glance, a single word, by making profit of the very smallest actions, by doing them all for love."

Spiritual Childhood

We don't have to make enormous changes in the world to find grace in our crosses. Especially when we are still recovering from the emotional and physical shocks of a cancer diagnosis, we can follow the example of St. Thérèse, who created a beautiful path called the "little way of spiritual childhood." Like a child, she focused her attention on performing tiny acts with deep love. "Jesus does not demand great deeds," she wrote. "He asks nothing from us but our love."

Ocean of Love

Many years after Thérèse's death, a woman named Agnes Gonxha Bojaxhiu followed in her footsteps and modeled her life on the little way of Thérèse. She began her ministry by picking up one dying person on the streets of Calcutta. It was a small action, and not very dramatic, but this woman, who was known as Mother Teresa, is remembered all over the world for her deep compassion and commitment to Christ.

Mother Teresa emphasized over and over that even if we can't do great deeds, we can still follow our beloved Jesus by performing little everyday acts of kindness. They can be as simple as complimenting someone's pretty dress, baking cookies for a housebound neighbor, or preparing a special meal for your family. Some people may be too ill to accomplish even the smallest thing, but that person can still pray, and prayer can change the world. The actions we do may seem like only a drop in the ocean, but without the drops, the ocean of love would disappear.

Helping others changes us, as the story of the robin reveals. The robin that tried to relieve Christ's suffering ended up with a beautiful red breast. It is true that the color came from blood, but there is still beauty there. As Christians, we know that darkness always gives way to light. The suffering of the crucifixion is surpassed by the joy of the resurrection. Jesus is the light of the world, and the love of our lives, and we can discover his presence in every situation, whether it is happy or sad. If we keep our eyes open, we will see evidence of his love and light everywhere.

Prayer

God, please pour out your grace upon me so that I may discover the talents you have given me that I may use in serving my neighbor. Help me to be patient with myself as I go through the healing process. Open my heart and my eyes to discover how there can be grace in my suffering and in the suffering of other people. Like the little robin, help me to remove thorns from the hearts of others. Amen.

Scriptural Reflections and Questions for Discussion

1. Read the passage at the beginning of the thirteenth chapter of John's gospel, where Jesus washes the disciples' feet. When you first read this passage, imagine that

Jesus is washing your feet. Reflect on the many times in your life that Jesus has ministered to you and loved you. In what ways is the Lord still washing your feet today?

2. Read the passage again. This time, imagine that you are washing Jesus' feet. Reflect on the people in your life whom you have ministered to and the ways you have helped them.

3. What are your gifts and talents? This question sometimes takes a while to answer, so if you are not sure now, that's fine. You can tuck the question away in the back of your mind and pray for an answer, and it will come. If you feel that you are aware of your gifts, how can you use them to minister to others?

4. Who are the people in your life who have found grace in the cross?

5. How have you found grace in cancer?

Exercise 1

This week, imagine that you are a little robin and remove one thorn from the life of someone who is burdened or suffering. Write about your experiences in your journal.

Exercise 2

If you are not feeling well enough to be very active this week, try removing thorns in others' lives by making a list of people who need help and praying for them.

Exercise 3

Turn every day into prayer by telling Jesus each morning, "I offer you the prayers, works, joys, and sufferings of this day. I offer you my heart."

Works Cited

Keating, Thomas. *Intimacy With God*. New York: Crossroad, 1994.

Lindbergh, Anne Morrow. *Gift From the Sea*. New York: Vintage Books, 1978.

Monahan, Molly. *Seeds of Grace: A Nun's Reflections on the Spirituality of Alcoholics Anonymous*. New York: Riverhead Books, 2001.

Mother Teresa. *No Greater Love*. Novato, CA: New World Library, 1997.

Nelson, John. *The Little Way of Saint Thérèse of Lisieux*. Liguori, MO: Liguori, 1997.

Nouwen, Henri J. M. *Bread for the Journey: A Day Book of Wisdom and Faith*. San Francisco: HarperSanFrancisco,1997.

Nouwen, Henri J. M. *Can You Drink the Cup?* Notre Dame, IN: Ave Maria Press, 1996.

Nouwen, Henri J. M. *The Inner Voice of Love: A Journey Through Anguish to Freedom*. New York: Image Books, 1998.

Nouwen, Henri J. M. *The Way of the Heart: Desert Spirituality and Contemporary Ministry*. New York: Ballantine Books, 1981.

Rawlings, Marjorie Kinnan. *Cross Creek*. New York: MacMillan Publishing Co., 1942.

St. Thérèse of Lisieux. *The Story of a Soul*. Translated by John Beevers. New York: Doubleday, 1989.

Stewart, Robert M. *Making Peace With Cancer: A Franciscan Journey*. Mahwah, NJ: Paulist Press, 2001.

Vann, Gerald. *The Pain of Christ and the Sorrow of God*. New York: Alba House, 1994.

Appendix

The Thread That Binds Us Together

Advice for Family and Friends of Women With Breast Cancer

A teddy bear with the seams coming apart. That's how I felt when I was first diagnosed with breast cancer on May 18, 2000. Although I continued with my daily life—washing clothes, preparing meals, combing my hair—inside I was cowering in fear. I had never felt so vulnerable.

My family and friends were the thread that kept me together. If it hadn't been for their many tender acts of love, I might have fallen into a dark well of despair. As the recipient of stunning acts of compassion, I've compiled some tips that may help you relate to a friend or relative with breast cancer.

The Diagnosis

Be a good listener. Your loved one will be facing a storm of emotional issues immediately following the diagnosis. Grief, anger, and depression may take turns raging in her heart. Don't feel you have to comment on every statement she makes. Don't think you have to "fix things" or make everything all right. Just sit quietly and let her talk or cry or shout. Try not to give advice about treatment options unless she asks you directly, "What would you do?"

Accept all her emotions. When I confided to a friend about how worried I was, she said, "Worried is OK," and gave me a hug. If your loved one gets angry, avoid saying, "There's nothing to be angry about." Just let the feelings flow. And keep in mind that some women will cry their hearts out, while others may not.

Be there. If you live nearby, call ahead to see how your friend is doing and if she wants company. Bring her lunch or supper. If you live too far to visit, call frequently. My sister Rosemary called me every day, and the sound of her voice was enormously comforting.

Show your love. Don't be shy about expressing your feelings. One friend hugged me and said, "We'll get through this." That plural pronoun warmed my heart.

Avoid the horror stories. Well-meaning friends and family members sometimes tell women with cancer stories that frighten them. Avoid these stories at all costs. If you are feeling especially anxious and fearful, try to avoid pouring out your emotions on your beloved. She is dealing with a storm of emotions on her own. Instead, find support somewhere else, either in a support group at your church or a local hospital, or through talks with your pastor.

Pray. Some women like to pray with others, while others prefer to pray alone. Ask your friend if she would like you to visit her and pray with her. Assure her that you are praying for her every day. Add her to your prayer list at church, and ask others to remember her in their prayers too.

After Surgery

Send cards and call often. A mailbox overflowing with get-well cards can be very therapeutic. I propped up all my cards in the living room and kept them there for the seven weeks of my radiation therapy. They became little emblems of love that lit up the room.

Keep the hugs coming. If you live close enough to visit, stop by with a hug and a smile. Take your cues from her. Is she looking for distraction from her illness or does she want to talk about the illness? If she needs a listener, be attentive and give her the gift of listening. If she wants distraction, invite her to a movie, share a favorite video or book, or take her out on a picnic.

Deliver meals. Food seems to be a universal expression of love, and after my surgery, this was truer than ever. Your friend will appreciate your stopping by with a hot meal, a cluster of homemade brownies, or other treats. Attach cooking or microwave instructions to meals.

Offer to find support. If your friend or relative expresses interest in attending a support group for women with cancer, help her find one. You may also want to offer to accompany her on the first visit.

Don't lean on her. You may be experiencing great anguish over the diagnosis, but this is not a time to expect your beloved to give you emotional support. Instead, you may want to attend a support group for friends and relatives of people with cancer.

During Radiation Therapy or Chemotherapy

Never second-guess her. No matter what course of treatment she chooses, support her decision. Many women will have doubts, at some future time, about the type of treatment they chose. Assure her that she made the best choice for her at the time.

Keep the love flowing. Radiation and chemotherapy can be a dicey time for cancer patients because the initial emotional support may seem to be waning. Offer to go with your friend to radiation or chemotherapy, or to meet her afterward for a snack, if she feels like eating.

Help with errands and childcare. Instead of asking, "What can I do?" try to be more specific. Try "May I take you to a radiation therapy session?" or "I'm going to the grocery store. What do you need?" If your friend has children, offer to watch them for a few hours.

During Recovery

Be careful not to blame the victim. We all yearn to know what "caused" our loved one's illness. But avoid suggesting that your friend or relative is to blame. Don't hint that she stayed too long in a stressful job. Don't hint that she should not have taken birth control pills. Keep in mind that the causes of the cancers that women typically experience, such as breast, ovarian, cervical, and uterine cancer, are unknown.

Express your interest. Some people think that once the medical treatments are over, the crisis has passed. But the emotional repercussions of a cancer diagnosis can last a very long time. I cherish the friends who ask me, "How are you doing?" in a way that allows me to discuss not only my physical state but my emotional state as well.

Continue to listen. Women who have undergone a cancer diagnosis often face other biopsies and tests in the years following their treatments. These tests can be very anxiety-provoking, and the best thing you can do is listen, be reassuring, and perhaps offer to accompany your friend to the doctors' offices.

Keep praying. Keep her permanently on your prayer list, asking God for her spiritual, emotional, and physical healing, and for the strength to handle whatever she may face in the future.

LORRAINE V. MURRAY was born in Yonkers, New York, and grew up in Miami. She holds a Ph.D. in philosophy from the University of Florida and is the author of *Grace Notes* (Resurrection Press, 2002). Currently she writes a column called "Grace Notes" for the *Atlanta Journal-Constitution* and is a guest columnist with the *Georgia Bulletin* and *America* magazine. Her work also appears on the American Cancer Society website and on the Faithandvalues.com website.

A cancer survivor, Lorraine serves as a minister to the sick and homebound at St. Thomas More Church in Decatur, Georgia, where she has conducted prayer and discussion groups for women with cancer. She works part-time in the Pitts Theology Library at Emory University and lives with her husband, Jef, a wildlife artist, in Decatur.